Leadership for Change in Teacher Education

Leadership for Change in Teacher Education

Voices of Canadian Deans of Education

Edited by

Susan E. Elliott-Johns
Nipissing University, Ontario, Canada

SENSE PUBLISHERS
ROTTERDAM / BOSTON / TAIPEI

A C.I.P. record for this book is available from the Library of Congress.

ISBN 978-94-6209-930-2 (paperback)
ISBN 978-94-6209-931-9 (hardback)
ISBN 978-94-6209-932-6 (e-book)

Published by: Sense Publishers,
P.O. Box 21858,
3001 AW Rotterdam,
The Netherlands
https://www.sensepublishers.com/

Printed on acid-free paper

All rights reserved © 2015 Sense Publishers

No part of this work may be reproduced, stored in a retrieval system, or transmitted in any form or by any means, electronic, mechanical, photocopying, microfilming, recording or otherwise, without written permission from the Publisher, with the exception of any material supplied specifically for the purpose of being entered and executed on a computer system, for exclusive use by the purchaser of the work.

TABLE OF CONTENTS

Foreword   vii
Clare Kosnik

Acknowledgements   xi

Leadership for Change in Contemporary Teacher Education: Why a Focus on the Role of Deans of Education?   1
Susan E. Elliott-Johns

1. Together Today for Society's Future: Indigenous Teacher Education in the Yukon   7
Deborah Bartlette

2. The Impact of Differentiation on Teacher Education in Ontario   13
Fiona Blaikie

3. Le Restructuration du Programme en Éducation au Campus Saint-Jean de l'Université de l'Alberta: L'Importance du Rôle des Leaders du Milieu Académique   19
Laurent Cammarata, Martine Cavanagh & Yvette d'Entremont

3a. Restructuring the Teacher Education Program at the Campus Saint-Jean of the University of Alberta: The Importance of the Role of Academic Leaders   25
Laurent Cammarata, Martine Cavanagh & Yvette d'Entremont

4. Exploring Complexities of Leadership for Teacher Education   31
Heather E. Duncan

5. Reflections on Change Leadership in a Faith-based Teacher Education Program   37
Kimberly Franklin

6. Leading in the Twenty-first Century Learning Environment: Challenging the Deanship   43
Rosetta Khalideen

7. Teachers Who Live in Glass Houses Should Not Throw Stones: A Call for Urgent Reform of University Teacher Education   49
Jane E. Lewis

TABLE OF CONTENTS

8. New Technologies and Leadership Challenges for Teacher Education *Kris Magnusson*	55
9. Walking the Tightrope: Staying Upright in Turbulent Times *David Mandzuk*	61
10. Reflecting and Acting on Reflection and Action: Mobilizing Teacher Education for Social Justice *Ken W. McCluskey*	67
11. Working against the Grain: Leadership for 21st Century Teacher Education *James McNinch*	73
12. Challenge and Complexity in Landscapes of Change: Building Effective Partnerships *Jacqueline Muldoon*	81
13. Leading from Within *Karen Roland*	87
14. Teacher Educator and Dean: Challenges, Joys, Trials and Successes *Ann Sherman*	93
Coda: Insights Gleaned from the Voices of Deans in Education *Susan E. Elliott-Johns*	97
About the Contributors	107
Index	113

CLARE KOSNIK

FOREWORD

Teacher education is a complex process. It is even more demanding in a country like Canada that has a rich and diverse population, two official languages, schools in urban, rural, and remote areas, and Aboriginal communities with specific needs. If we are to serve the needs of our unique communities there is truly not a one-size-fits-all teacher education program. *Leadership for Change in Teacher Education: Voices of Canadian Deans of Education* is a wonderful collection of essays that provides many examples of strong teacher education programs where student teachers are prepared for both their local contexts and for the global education community.

Although written many years ago, Ducharme and Ducharme's (1996) observation still holds true that teacher education programs and faculty are viewed as "both the cause of all school problems and the source of many of its solutions" (p. 705). In this period of hyper-criticism of education, schools of education have come under unrelenting inspection by many stakeholders. However, the sheer complexity of teacher education is often not fully appreciated. For example, Goodwin and Kosnik (2013) contend: "Simply put, it is reasonable to assume that quality teacher preparation depends on quality teacher educators" (p. 334). However, the quality of teacher preparation also depends on the leadership of the school of education. An individual teacher educator no matter how charismatic, knowledgeable, and hard working cannot do it all, because becoming a teacher is not a straight-forward process. In order for student teachers to acquire the skills, knowledge, and dispositions they need for effective teaching they must be immersed in an entire teacher education program, one with a clear vision of good teaching and an understanding of the process of becoming a teacher. Deans of education play a pivotal role in establishing these conditions; through their leadership they help faculty shape the school's vision, develop programs to match it, and continually revise the program to ensure they are meeting the needs of the many stakeholders. The impact of the dean on students and faculty cannot be underestimated.

Leadership is demanding anyway but is made ever more so in our increasingly politicized context. The criticisms of teacher education programs abound and it is often the deans who are the "face" of the institution. They are required to respond to seemingly never-ending demands. Ironically, deans of education as individuals are often overlooked in the rush to improve education, implement mandates, shore up sagging finances, attend to the concerns of stakeholders, and on and on. Susan Elliott-Johns recognized this void in the literature which led to her compiling and

FOREWORD

editing *Leadership for Change in Teacher Education: Voices of Canadian Deans of Education*. This is a laudable goal which she fulfilled admirably by presenting a unique text that provides insider's stories of the work of deans of education. This collection of essays highlights the work of 14 highly committed individuals all of whom are working in demanding situations. Giving them a voice deepens our understanding of the complexity of leading a school of education and adds another piece of the "puzzle" of teacher education.

In the midst of public critiques of education, deans of education are charged with guiding their faculty and students through the choppy waters of competing demands and unrealistic expectations. This is not an easy task and it is made all the more difficult because we so often think of deans as just administrators but they are so much more. How do we get a sense of them? Aidan Chambers (1985) notes that, "storying ... defines humanity and makes us human" (p. 3). He observes "in one way or another we tell ourselves and each other stories about life" (p. 4). Stories are powerful because they engage the reader in ways that typical and traditional academic literature does not. Against the backdrop of a highly politicized educational context I found the deans' stories in this volume compelling; by including both personal and professional stories they gave me a sense of the individuals—their struggles, their joys, their challenges, and their personal goals. By bringing together many threads of their lives the stories gave me a peek behind the scenes.

I was struck by the hopeful tone of each author. Although they recount a crushing workload with much of their work invisible there is an optimism present in each essay. These veteran educators have seen it all in their careers yet they have not lost their love for education or their sense of hope. Throughout the chapters it is clear that these deans are not settling for the "just a program," approach; they are aiming for great programs—high achievement by students, productive faculty, and a healthy relationship with neighbouring communities. Yes these are lofty goals, but the essays here include many examples of innovations actually implemented in their programs to meet the challenges of teaching and learning in the twenty-first century. It is clearly evident that they care deeply about their faculty and students. Their caring stance and outstanding leadership skills lend further support to Ducharme and Ducharme's claim that teacher educators can provide solutions to problems of education. This compelling text sheds light on unsung heroes of education whose work is making a difference. I know I will never again think of a dean as *just* an administrator!

REFERENCES

Chambers, A. (1985). *Booktalk: Occasional writing on literature and children*. London, UK: The Bodley Head.

Ducharme, E., & Ducharme, M. (1996). Development of the teacher education professoriate. In F. Murray (Ed.), *The teacher educator's handbook: Building a knowledge base for the preparation of teachers* (pp. 691-714). San Francisco, CA: Jossey-Bass.

Goodwin. L. A., & Kosnik, C. (2013). Quality teacher educators = quality teachers?: Conceptualizing essential domains of knowledge for those who teach teachers. *Teacher Development: An International Journal of Teachers' Professional Development, 17*, 334-346.

Clare Kosnik
OISE/University of Toronto
Canada

ACKNOWLEDGEMENTS

Leadership for Change in Teacher Education is the result of a collaborative writing project with deans of education across Canada—all of whom carved out precious time in their already busy professional lives to contribute reflections on the topic and to provoke further thinking about contemporary leadership for teacher education and change. It has been a pleasure and a privilege to work with all of these colleagues, from coast to coast, as the project took shape.

I would like to thank all the authors who so generously agreed to share their collective wisdom, insights and lived experiences. The ongoing investments of time, energy, expertise and passion for leadership, learning and teaching resonate throughout the authentic voices captured in this text. I am also very grateful for everyone's patience and tenacity throughout the writing process: Enthusiasm for, and engagement in, the project never waned. This too was much appreciated—and essential to completion of the project. Thank you for all of your support, encouragement, and shared passion for teacher education, leadership and change.

Special thanks must also go to Teri-Ann McDonald whose meticulous attention to detail was invaluable during the final preparation of the manuscript.

Last but not least, my sincere thanks are extended to family, friends and colleagues who, in ways too numerous to mention here, all continue to sustain what has become my life's work: teacher education research and practice.

Susan E. Elliott-Johns

SUSAN E. ELLIOTT-JOHNS

LEADERSHIP FOR CHANGE IN CONTEMPORARY TEACHER EDUCATION

Why a Focus on the Role of Deans of Education?

The post-secondary education sector is currently experiencing significant transition and change as technological innovation, financial constraints, and shifting demographics (to name but a few significant factors) continue to create climates of uncertainty and precarity. While governments, university leaders, and other stakeholders expound the need for positive change, in the face of current uncertainties, it is often difficult to move ahead without reliable input from sector participants. Furthermore, it seems, input is often deemed hard to obtain or not sought out at all.

Being part of this post-secondary landscape, faculties of education across Canada (and around the world) are also engaged in significant transitions and change as the expectations for, and understandings of, teacher education and the teaching profession experience intense scrutiny and increasing commentary under the banner "teacher education reform." Educational change, including teacher education change, is political, multi-faceted, and uncertain; bringing about change also takes time and skilled leadership. The purpose of this book was to invite, compile and publish a collection of brief but engaging and provocative essays from deans of education across Canada, in order to share their ideas and perspectives on leadership for change in contemporary teacher education. Taken separately, each essay in this unique collection explores critical issues and offers rich insights relevant to navigating the complex demands of leadership for 21st century teacher education. Collectively, the essays present an illuminating collage of insider's voices on a topic that has a very limited profile in the literature.

As leaders, deans of education must mediate between administration and faculty and, as a result, are called upon to wear many hats daily. For example, in addition to responsibilities for academic leadership and scholarship, "hats" worn may include administrative manager, resource coordinator, community builder, fundraiser, mentor, team builder et al. Very few studies looking at the "leadership journeys" of deans of education (Bowen, 1995) have been undertaken, and Gmelch, Wolverton, Wolverton, and Sarros (1999) wrote, "The academic deanship is the least studied and most misunderstood position in the academy." This situation does not appear to have changed very much almost fifteen years later. A comprehensive search of current literature revealed very few relevant citations beyond those of Cole, Elijah, and Knowles (1998), Jackson (2000), and Gmelch

S.E. Elliott-Johns (ed.), Leadership for Change in Teacher Education, 1–6.
© 2015 Sense Publishers. All rights reserved.

(2002)—and, it should be noted, all of these were published more than a decade ago. As John Loughran (2014) writes, "Because teacher education is ubiquitous and an integral component of education systems world-wide, concentration on the organization of teacher education has overshadowed the development of deeper understandings of those that work within the system" (p. vii). While Loughran is referring primarily to teacher educators here, the voices of deans of education (who frequently, if not always, possess background as teacher educators and provide leadership in faculties of teacher education), might also offer insights and deepen understandings about the nature of their "work within the system." Specific aspects of the role of the dean pertaining to management and leadership for change in teacher education comprise the focus of all contributed essays in this volume.

Therefore, this project sought to surface current insights from responses to the following question from multiple perspectives and locations across Canada: In the current era of teacher education reform, what kinds of lived experience might deans of education share to assist others in understanding their role as leaders of teacher education and change? In other words, what does it means to be a dean of education in the 21st century? What can be learned by listening to the voices of deans of education in terms of better understanding the nature of their work in relation to leadership for teacher education, especially in the current context of significant transitions, change, and uncertainty?

As leaders of change in university contexts where initial teacher education takes place, deans of education have considerable capacity to inform and enhance the discourse on teacher education change and, I believe, it is essential that their voices are heard. Using an *emic* (or insider) perspective approach to draw on "behavior or beliefs that are meaningful for the participant" (Savin-Baden & Howell Major, 2013, p. 12), these essays offer increased understandings of a range of perspectives on leadership for contemporary teacher education, and the research, practice, pedagogy, and institutional change currently informing (and, at times, driving) the leadership of the sixteen contributing authors.

Malone's (2013) work, *Leading Educational Change: Global Issues, Challenges, and Lessons on Whole-System Reform*, provoked further reflection on leadership for change in teacher education. A recurring notion was how very seldom we actually seem to hear from deans of education on prevalent "big picture" issues (other than, perhaps, our own dean, if we happen to work in a faculty of education?) In the present geo-political climate, there are probably many reasons why this is the case. However, the omission of such knowledgeable "voices from the field" (in their capacity as teacher educators and leaders of teacher education) not only from the public domain, but also from crucial systemic decision-making processes, is becoming increasingly problematic—particularly when decisions being made will continue to have long-lasting implications for teacher education, teacher educators, teachers, and, by association, their students. Where, I wondered, were the research conversations interrogating fundamental and complex changes related to teacher education reform currently being experienced in faculties of education all across Canada? Conversations that include the voices of deans of education?

Another catalyst in the conceptualizing of this project was a recent article in a professional journal, entitled "Deans Speak Out" (Pitt, Dibbon, Sumara, & Wiens, 2014). In this article, four deans of education from across the country were asked to comment on changes in 21st century teacher education in relation to meeting the teaching and learning demands of this new century. Each of the deans responded quite differently to the question of how faculties of education should respond to changes in the profession of teaching through their pre-service programs. As I read, I found myself thinking I'd like to hear much more on this topic—and to have an opportunity to "listen in" on the voices of other deans of education too. Consequently, the central goal of this project became a focus on the voices of leaders from faculties of education across Canada: making available valuable insights from their shared reflections on, for example, vision(s) for contemporary teacher education; complexities inherent in their leadership roles; pedagogy and practice for teacher education; pressing internal and external conditions (including incessant calls for accountability); collaboration and continuous engagement with all stakeholders.

While related in terms of the common enterprise of educating students and teachers, in reality, school systems and faculties of education operate in different situated contexts. That said, understanding educational change as "inevitably a political process that has a tendency to be episodic, driven by external policies, susceptible to electoral cycles, and reactive to outside pressures" (Malone, 2013, p. 129) appears to be increasingly as relevant to faculties of education today as it is to the school systems where graduates of teacher education will apply to teach. Broadly speaking, educational change, including teacher education change, is undoubtedly political, multi-faceted, uncertain; it takes time, skilled leadership, and, furthermore:

> positive educational change is possible when it is embedded in a clear vision, strong leadership, resource investment, internal and external accountability, high-quality practice, collaboration, and continuous engagement by all stakeholders. (Malone, 2013, p. 2)

The question thus became, "What would we hear from deans of education invited to share their perspectives on leadership for change in contemporary teacher education?" This collection of essays is the result of pursuing answers to that very question. Inspired by Malone's challenge to other global leaders in education, I invited leaders of faculties of education from across Canada to reflect on the research, policies and practices currently informing leadership and change in teacher education. I, too, asked them to encapsulate their thinking by writing a brief essay of approximately 2000 words. In essence, participants were asked to contribute to a forum that would share reflections on questions related to five broad themes relevant to the topic under study. More specifically, the deans were asked to respond in relation to their own situated leadership for contemporary teacher education. The five broad themes were presented in the initial invitation as the following guiding questions:

- What critical issues, research, and current ways of thinking about teaching, learning and pedagogy for teacher education inform your leadership of a faculty of education?
- What are the most important external/internal conditions and inherent tensions encountered in your work?
- What insights can you share about the ways contemporary thinking about teacher education and change are reflected in pre-service programs at your current location?
- What important changes, transitions, transformations are you experiencing in leadership for teacher education?
- What is your vision for teacher education, going forward?

Fourteen completed essays resulted from the many prompt and positive responses received from deans of education, literally, from coast to coast. Several leaders immediately embraced the opportunity and committed to contributing an essay on the topic. In fact, the proposed project generated considerable excitement and enthusiasm in my in-box. For example:

Hello Susan.

Thank-you for your invitation. As I complete my 6 year tenure as Dean of Education, this exercise will provide me a golden opportunity to reflect on critical issues of Leadership in and the changing landscape of teacher education. I will have an abstract to you by the end of the month. This seems like a wonderful project ....

Good morning, Susan.

Thank you for your invitation to contribute to such an interesting collection. I will have an abstract to you by the 21st as requested.

Hello Susan,

I am very interested in this opportunity and will do my best to get an abstract to you by February 21. I am not only passionate about this topic, I think I have led through some "interesting times" and circumstances at (***) that maybe provide me with some thoughts, and insight on this .... I share all of this precisely because I think it provides me with insights to some of the questions posed ....

It sounds like a great project. Even if I don't participate, I will read this with interest!

Dear Susan,

Thanks for the invitation to submit an essay for publication in your edited text. I think a book of the nature you are proposing is timely granted the changing [and chaotic] landscape of teacher education and education in general. I would be pleased to write an essay and just need to further contemplate what my focus will be. I will try to send you the abstract by the required deadline.

All busy people, these four (and many other deans) grasped the challenge right away and made time in their hectic schedules to meet rigorous expectations and tight timelines in order to participate in the project—for which I continue to be very grateful. The list of essay titles in the "Table of Contents" offers a glimpse into the breadth and depth of interpretations of the topic and different directions taken in responses to the theme of leadership for teacher education. Clearly, there is much for us to consider and learn from these voices about where (and how) teacher education takes place and who is leading the education faculty. Furthermore, what do these voices convey about contemporary visions of "preferred futures" (Magnusson, 2014) for teacher education?

The first-hand knowledge and rich expertise deans can offer in-house as leaders of teacher education, in addition to perspectives on relevant research and policy for teacher education broadly speaking, frequently appears to be underestimated as a source of critical insights for policymakers and others responsible for making decisions about the future direction of teacher education. All fourteen of the essays here resonate with knowledge and expertise gained from experience in the field, draw attention to *emic* (or insider) perspectives on leadership practices that endeavour to inform and improve pedagogy for contemporary teacher education, and raise critical questions going forward. Whether taken together or read as stand-alone pieces, these explorations of nuanced approaches to navigating the complex challenges and opportunities encountered in their work as deans of education make for compelling reading. They also provoke further reflection and increased understandings of leadership for change.

As a result of actively engaging with insights shared in this collage of resonant voices, readers might promote further critical discussion and increased understandings of the role of the dean in leadership for teacher education and change in their own geographical location and/or institutional context. The text offers a highly accessible resource for education decision makers, practitioners/teacher education researchers, and interested policymakers—all stakeholders who have the capacity to invite informed voices from the field to the table, thus actively enhancing meaningful discussion and informing decision-making processes from multiple perspectives.

Wepner, D'Onofrio, and Wilhite (2008) concluded, "Effectiveness in the deanship is a combination of the person and the institutional culture" (p. 166). As the voices presented in this rich sampling of diverse perspectives on leadership for change will demonstrate, the knowledge, expertise, and aptitudes of these deans of education clearly reside in advocating wisely today for the future of teacher education tomorrow.

REFERENCES

Bowen, L. S. (Ed.). (1995). *The wizards of odds: Leadership journeys of education deans*. Washington, DC: American Association of Colleges for Teacher Education.

Cole, A. L., Elijah, R., & Knowles, G. (Eds.). (1998). *The heart of the matter: Teacher educators and teacher education reform*. San Francisco, CA: Caddo Gap Press.

Gmelch, W. H. (Ed.). (2002). *Deans' balancing acts: Education leaders and the challenges they face*. Washington, DC: American Association of Colleges for Teacher Education.

Gmelch, W. H., Wolverton, M., Wolverton, M. L., & Sarros, J. C. (1999). The academic dean: An imperiled species searching for balance. *Research in Higher Education, 40*, 717-740.

Jackson, J. F. L. (2000). *Decanal work: Using role theory and the sociology of time to study the executive behavior of college of education deans*. Unpublished doctoral dissertation. Ames, IA: Iowa State University.

Loughran, J. (2014). Series editor's foreword. In M. Lunenberg, J. Dengerink, & F. Kotrthagen (Eds.), *The professional teacher educator: Roles, behaviour, and professional development of teacher educators* (pp. vii-ix). Rotterdam, the Netherlands: Sense.

Magnusson, K. (2014). Innovation, technology and teacher education. In S. E. Elliott-Johns (Ed.), *Leadership for change in contemporary teacher education: Voices of Canadian deans of education* (this volume, pp. 55-59). Rotterdam, the Netherlands: Sense.

Malone, H. J. (Ed.). (2013). *Leading educational change: Global issues, challenges, and lessons on whole-system reform*. New York, NY: Teachers College Press.

Pitt, A., Dibbon, D., Sumara, D., & Wiens, J. R. (2014). Deans speak out. *Education Canada, 54*(1). Retrieved from http://www.cea-ace.ca/education-canada/article/deans-speak-out

Savin-Baden, M., & Howell Major, C. (2013). *Qualitative research: The essential guide to theory and practice*. New York, NY: Routledge.

Wepner, S. B., D'Onofrio, A., & Wilhite, S. C. (2008). The leadership dimensions of education deans. *Journal of Teacher Education, 59*, 153-169.

Susan E. Elliott-Johns
Schulich School of Education
Nipissing University
Ontario, Canada

DEBORAH BARTLETTE

1. TOGETHER TODAY FOR SOCIETY'S FUTURE

Indigenous Teacher Education in the Yukon

INTRODUCTION

The Yukon is a unique context for Indigenous education in Canada. Most First Nations are self-governing; there are no reserves or reserve schools. Nonetheless, FN students have less educational success in the K-12 system than their non-FN counterparts in the same classrooms and schools. Self-determination and educational success go hand-in-hand. We need to pursue a model of teacher education in the Yukon and all of Canada which creates teachers of Indigenous and non-Indigenous background who can integrate Indigenous understandings and knowledge into their curriculum and teaching. In this way, we can build a just educational system for all students.

BACKGROUND AND CONTEXT

Forty years ago, a group of First Nations leaders from the Yukon travelled to Ottawa to present a document to then Prime Minister Pierre Trudeau. Impatient, and rightfully so, with the social and economic issues faced by Yukon First Nations, the Yukon Native Brotherhood wrote *Together Today for Our Children Tomorrow* (1973), thus setting out a vision for a just future which would enable full participation by Yukon First Nations in the dominant society. They were not asking for handouts but for opportunity and challenged government to truly hear what they were saying. First Nations in the Yukon never had treaties and at the time, the Territory was fully managed by the federal government. The Yukon Native Brotherhood wanted to build a society in which Indigenous people were full citizens with full rights and responsibilities, to enable all people in the Yukon to work together for the benefit of everyone.

However, *Together Today* took the bold step of setting out the conditions needed for full participation and equality by Indigenous people, a model that would inform future self-governing agreements, one that remains a model today for Indigenous self-determination. "If we are successful, the day will come when ALL Yukoners will be proud of our Heritage and Culture and will respect our Indian identity. Only then will we be equal Canadian brothers [sic]" (p. 16). *Together Today* asks that First Nations peoples, culture, language and tradition be as equally valued as European culture and that First Nations people control their own destiny. Summing up the situation for First Nations people at the time, they wrote: "We are being brainwashed that White is right and Indian is wrong ..." (p. 16). "We must have the right to be different and the right to be accepted as fellow citizens and fellow human beings. Most of the time, the Whiteman has insisted that we become instant Whitemen. This was never possible" (p. 18). "With a just settlement of our claims, we feel we can participate as equals and then we will be able to live together as neighbours" (p. 16). "We want to take part in the development of the Yukon and Canada, not stop it. But we can only participate as Indians. We will not sell our heritage for a quick buck" (p. 18).

Together Today provided the foundation for the self-government agreements currently in place for 11 or 14 Yukon First Nations. Self-government has created a unique context for Indigenous people and thus Indigenous education in the Yukon. Self-government for Yukon First Nations means settled land claims, their own governments and control of their own resources, including funds for economic development, health and social services and education. First Nations (there are few Metis or Inuit in the Yukon) make up 25% of the population. There are no reserves in the Yukon and no reserve or band schools. First Nations students attend the same schools as their non-First Nations counterparts and per student funding for First Nations students is no different than for non-First Nations students. As in other parts of Canada, the legacy of residential schools is writ large upon the Indigenous population.

In spite of self-government, First Nations students continue to experience less educational success than their non-First Nations counterparts, particularly in rural communities. We must ask ourselves why, in spite of self-government and self-determination, First Nations students in the same K-12 schools as non-First Nations students still have lower levels of educational achievement. Perhaps we need to look beyond self-determination, as important as that is, and focus on the educational system itself. In spite of efforts towards Indigenization of our programs and institutions, is there something inherent in our system which de-privileges Indigenous learners? De France (2013) states that "academia has a long-standing tradition of designing and delivering courses in a way that favours Eurocentric ways of knowing and being, claiming that if people want to succeed, they must adapt to this variant of teaching and learning" (p. 87). When we are training teachers in the academic tradition, how can we expect them to teach differently in their own classrooms?

Education is key to fully realizing the vision set out in *Together Today* which makes educational achievement for First Nations all the more important. The direct connection between education and economic participation is clear and important; the role of education in having all people understand and value Indigenous culture is a bigger challenge. Certainly strides have been made. Yukon College delivers the Yukon Native Teacher (YNTEP) education program, one of many such programs offered by the university of Regina (among others) that has increased the number of Indigenous teachers in public schools, First Nations departments of education and the Yukon government department of education. The program is also open to non-First Nations students. As a result, non-Indigenous pre-service teachers build a solid understanding of First Nations history, values and culture studying side-by-side with their First Nations colleagues—a small part of the vision expressed in *Together Today*. The program incorporates Indigenous values and cultural understanding through on the land culture camps taught with the involvement of elders.

However, even these programs do not go far enough in providing meaningful integration of Indigenous epistemology. If we cannot provide teacher education programs which model this integration, how can we expect ALL teachers, both Indigenous and non-Indigenous, to lead their own classrooms and develop curriculum in ways that realize the goals of *Together Today*? These goals are not simply nice sentiments, but critical to addressing historic wrongs and furthering the work of creating a more just society for Indigenous people.

Marie Battiste (2002) writes:

> Canada's educational institutions have largely ignored and continue to ignore Indigenous knowledge and pedagogy. It is clear that the exclusive use of Eurocentric knowledge has failed First Nations children. However, despite this realization ... few teacher training institutions have developed any insight into the legal, political and cultural foundations of Aboriginal people, often treating Indigenous knowledge as if it were a matter of multi-cultural and cross-cultural education. (p. xx)

This is, in my opinion, an important point. Indigenous people are not simply another thread in Canada's multicultural tapestry; colonialism and Eurocentric education are examples of the inherent hegemonic tendencies of our society reinforced and reproduced by our educational systems. Thus teaching (at all levels), developing curricula and even administering programs are political acts. We as educators, especially as educators of teachers, have a particular responsibility and obligation to critically reflect on what we do.

Critical pedagogy is well known within educational contexts. Paulo Friere, Henri Giroux, bell hooks and Michael Apple are familiar names frequently cited in any number of graduate papers. But in practice, has post-secondary education itself turned a critical eye to its own pedagogy and practice? Eric Margolis would say "No." Margolis's series of essays, *The Hidden Curriculum in Higher Education* (2001), written by and for post-secondary educators, turns the critical pedagogy lens onto the post-secondary world and suggests that universities and colleges are guilty of producing gender, race and class hierarchies which support society's inequalities. We produce programs and curricula that, in spite of our academic expertise and best intentions (in most cases), have not critically examined what is included and what is not. The exclusion of Indigenous knowledge is a clear example of hidden curriculum which becomes doubly problematic in teacher education. Battiste (2002) writes that it is time for educators to reaffirm, as the courts have, the right of Aboriginal people to have their rights respected and protected:

> The task then, is to sensitize the western consciousness of Canadians in general and educators in particular to the colonial and neo-colonial practices that continue to marginalize and racialize Aboriginal students and to the

unique rights and relationships Aboriginal people have in their homeland ... educators must be made aware of the existing interpretative monopoly of Eurocentric education and learn how the fundamental political processes of Canada have been laced with racism. (p. 10)

These are extremely hard questions to ask ourselves. We want to believe that we are good people (particularly if we are educators) who think long and hard about ethical practice. However, if we are to live up to our ideals, we must ask ourselves these hard questions and be prepared for even harder-to-hear answers. In my own teaching of graduate students in education, many of whom are already practicing educators, their graduate studies are often the first time they encounter the concept of critical examination of one's own practices (teaching, curriculum) and philosophies for hidden hegemony. This should not be the case. Rather, all of us should be regularly practicing rigorous, critical self-reflection, focusing on the "why" of what we have chosen to do and not to do in our teaching, to include and not include in our curriculum and program planning. We spend considerable time on the "what" and "how" and not enough on the processes by which we made these decisions in the first place.

Which brings us full-circle and back to the vision set out for Indigenous people in the Yukon in *Together Today*. More than 40 years ago they recognized the key role of education in the journey to making full equality a reality for First Nations peoples. It is only through education that ALL people will come to understand Indigenous history, tradition and culture as equal. The education system, through residential schools, was originally used to try and wipe out Indigenous identity. Thus the current education system, including teacher education, has particular responsibility to right this wrong. Furthermore, this goes beyond cross-cultural training; it requires deep critical reflection and a hard look at the foundations of our contemporary curricula. By critically examining our own programs, curricula and practice with an eye to decolonization, we also begin to address issues of hegemony and working towards a more just society for everyone.

Forty years ago, Yukon First Nations leadership marched on Ottawa to demand acknowledgment of their inherent rights as Indigenous people. They wished to fully participate in society to build a better future for everyone's children, Indigenous and non-Indigenous. We in the Yukon continue to work towards fully achieving that vision. It is a vision that is important for all of Canada and Canadian society: In essence, by working together to create more just educational systems, we can contribute to a more just society, for the benefit of everyone's children.

There are no quick or easy answers to these important questions. Systems have a life of their own and are difficult to change. A student of mine ended a recent paper with a few lines by the German poet Maria Rainer Rilke which feel very apropos here:

Be patient toward all that is unsolved in your heart and try to love the questions themselves, like locked rooms and like books that are now written in a very foreign tongue. ... And the point is, to live everything. Live the questions now. Perhaps you will then gradually, without noticing it, live along some distant day into the answer.

Where better to begin unlocking the rooms than teacher education programs?

REFERENCES

Battiste, M. (2002). *Indigenous knowledge and pedagogy in First Nations education: A literature review with recommendations.* Ottawa, ON: Indian and Northern Affairs Canada. Retrieved from http://www.afn.ca/uploads/files/education/24._2002_oct_marie_battiste_indigenousknowledgeandpedagogy_lit_review_for_min_working_group.pdf

De France, M. (2013). Indigenous/Aboriginal pedagogies restored: Courses and programs in the faculty of education at the University of Victoria. *International Education, 43*(1), 85-100.

Margolis, E. (Ed.). (2001). *The hidden curriculum in higher education.* New York/London: Routledge Press.

Yukon Native Brotherhood/Council of Yukon First Nations. (1973). *Together today for our children tomorrow.* Retrieved from www.cyfn.ca/together-today-for-our-children-tomorrow

Deborah Bartlette
Yukon College
Vice-President, Academic and Student Services
Former Dean, Yukon Native Education Teacher Education Program
Yukon, Canada

FIONA BLAIKIE

2. THE IMPACT OF DIFFERENTIATION ON TEACHER EDUCATION IN ONTARIO

INTRODUCTION

It is spring 2014, and teacher education in Ontario is the midst of epic change.

Policy based regulations and laws versus guidelines are entirely different. It is relatively easy to create agreements in the form of guidelines or accords. One such example is the high level Accord on Initial Teacher Education created by the Association of Canadian Deans of Education (2005). Policy, law, and regulations demand compliance in practice.

Ontario teacher education programs currently operate out of 13[i] publically funded universities. In part a legacy of the Mike Harris government, non-publically funded teacher education is offered as well in Ontario via cross-border universities such as Charles Sturt University (Australia), as well as those operating under special Ministerial Consent such as Redeemer University College.

My essay focuses on the impact of government legislated change on publically funded universities. Players include the deans of the 13 publically funded universities, the Ontario Teachers' Federation (OTF); the Ministry of Education, and the Ministry of Training, Colleges and Universities (MTCU) which creates legislation and policy in relation to funding universities and colleges. Finally, the Ontario College of Teachers (OCT) plays a key role in teacher education. OCT was created under the Mike Harris government and it has the power and authority under the Ontario College of Teachers Act, 1996, Ontario Regulation 347/02 to accredit teacher education programs in Ontario. OCT certifies teachers from beyond Ontario, and also makes judgments about "fitness to practice" (Ontario College of Teachers Act, 1996a).

POLICY ON DIFFERENTIATION

A pivotal influence on current Liberal party MTCU policy with regard to colleges and universities is the Higher Education Quality Council of Ontario or HEQCO, "an agency of the government of Ontario" (Weingarten & Deller, 2010, p.2). HEQCO's purpose is to provide government with informed opinions to guide policy decisions. Since 2010, MTCU has been considering differentiation, commissioning HEQCO's *The Benefits of Greater Differentiation of Ontario's University Sector*. In July 2013, HEQCO published *A Data Set to Inform the Differentiation Discussion*. Moodie (2013) writing in *University Affairs* describes

S.E. Elliott-Johns (ed.), Leadership for Change in Teacher Education, 13–18.
© 2015 Sense Publishers. All rights reserved.

this study as flawed because it measures or groups "Ontario universities on only one dimension, research intensity."

The impact of differentiation is that universities are identified differently. This is about categorizing and branding each university, and extends to issues of mission, vision, scope and purpose. The HEQCO variables impacting differentiation include research intensity, teaching focus, and focus on graduate and/or undergraduate programs. Enshrined in Acts, typically, Canadian university governance is bi-cameral, via Boards of Trustees (or Governors) and Senate. Universities promote the dissemination of knowledge (teaching) and the production of new knowledge (research). Research and graduate programs are closely aligned because it is through research that we engage in training graduate students. Indeed, I would argue that all universities privilege research, otherwise they are not universities. They do this, for example, via tenure and promotion, annual reports and merit. While processes are different in each university, service, teaching and research are key elements of the work of scholars.

Key to government achieving differentiation has been to require each university to submit "strategic mandate agreements" or SMAs, which were due in to MTCU by Christmas of 2013. SMAs require each university to identify areas of strength. These would then impact funding, programs, hiring, and thus potentially all faculty, staff and students. Some SMAs may have identified teacher education as a priority; this would depend on internal priorities and politics. Everything, after all, is special. The outcomes of the SMA process have yet to be realized, and will be impacted by the outcome of the June 2014 election. There are potentially massive impacts for publically funded universities as a whole, internally and externally, politically, pedagogically, and fiscally.

TEACHER EDUCATION AND DIFFERENTIATION

The focus for deans of education in spring 2013 was much anticipated change to teacher education. Yet to be announced formally by MTCU, these changes were discussed in the context of an oversupply of teachers from public and private universities. As a result, deans of education learnt that enrolment might be cut and capped, programs and practicum days lengthened. With no formal regulations in place, it was announced in the spring of 2013 that in the fall a Program Change Agreement (PCA) would need to be submitted to and then negotiated with MTCU including program elements, a transition plan, funding and enrolment. In a university setting where change typically is turgid because of internal consultation processes and multiple levels of governance and associated approvals, deans were concerned about timing. Many of us worried that Ministry had not yet undertaken a cost analysis of changes. Overall, it seemed that there was little understanding of the impact of this, internally and externally. Impact is context dependent, given that each of the 13 universities is uniquely different in terms of age, location, size, and program foci.

On June 5th 2013, the announcement came via the media, and here I cite the *Globe and Mail*. Alphonso, Morrow, and Bradshaw (2013) announced that all changes would be required to be in effect at all 13 publically funded Ontario universities by the start of the academic year in 2015. There would be a major funding cut. Each BIU (basic income unit—the amount paid to fund each student) would be cut from 2.0 BIUs per student to 1.5. Each program would have its enrolment cut in half and capped. Program length would be increased from two terms to four; practicum would double in length from 40 days to 80. The fiscal impact would be massive:

> Ontario will cut the number of new teachers who graduate every year in half and increase the length of time it takes them to complete a degree, The Globe and Mail has learned. The move is aimed at curbing the growing glut of would-be teachers who cannot find work in their field—not only in Ontario, but in several other regions of the country. It is also designed to keep Ontario-trained teachers competitive with their counterparts in other provinces and countries, who follow longer courses of study...The change, which is set to roll out by September, 2015, is expected to be announced Wednesday by Education Minister Liz Sandals and Training, Colleges and Universities Minister Brad Duguid .... The Ontario College of Teachers certifies 11,000 new teachers every year, of whom roughly 7,500 come from faculties of education within the province. (Alphonso, Morrow, & Bradshaw, 2013)

The funding and enrolment cuts will have a fourfold impact: The cut by 25% to BIU funding per student; no increase to tuition for teacher education mandated by MTCU (though tuition at private universities is not regulated); an increase in program and practicum length and therefore costs, and halving the number of students. For some universities, faculties of education provide significant income (based on BIUs and tuition). Executive Heads lobbied behind the scenes discussing implications with one another, internally, and with ministry officials. Smaller programs were now, potentially, in jeopardy. Large well-funded programs were less so. For each of us, our university context is unique, with associated challenges.

In November 2013 my decanal colleagues and I sent representatives to work with OCT on new accreditation procedures and the new OCT guide that would address the changes to program content and length, as well as practicum. The new program was integrated via Ontario College of Teachers Regulation 283/13 OCT, 1996, then approved October 23 2013; published via e-laws October 25 2013; published in the Ontario Gazette on November 9 2013 amending O. Reg 347/02 which is now revoked and substituted by the requirement that practicum is a minimum of 80 days in length; the program is four semesters long; program design is "consistent with and reflects the College's 'Standards of Practice for the Teaching Profession' and 'Ethical Standards for the Teaching Profession,' 'current research in teacher education' and 'the integration of theory and practice in teacher education'" (Ontario College of Teachers Act, 1996b). The Regulation describes compliance procedures required for the implementation date of September 2015.

Over the fall and winter of 2013-2014 the deans of education told one another of our plans for expanded two-year programs of two terms each, or consecutive four term programs. Some of us were considering disbanding concurrent education entirely; others believe that concurrent education must remain a staple, for internal funding and pedagogical reasons. Critically important vocational education in the form of technology education programs are in danger of being disbanded widely due to the very high cost of delivery. Other areas of specialization such as Intermediate Senior science and Aboriginal education are in jeopardy due to loss of critical capacity. Given the tight funding envelopes for BIU funded graduate spaces we were told by MTCU colleagues that it would not be possible at all for any of us to re-create our B.Ed degree programs as M.Ed or M.Teaching degree programs (in the context of our own M.Ed and doctoral programs, and two relatively small M. Teaching programs at the Ontario Institute for Studies in Education at the University of Toronto (OISE UT) where the teaching components are accredited by OCT).

However, on May 1st 2014, shortly after the release of the Provincial Budget by Premier Wynne, articles published in the *Star* and *Globe and Mail* newspapers announced that OISE UT would be replacing its B.Ed program with the M.Teaching program, funded at 3 BIUs per student. Of course their enrolment would be cut in half. The M.Teaching would include the program elements required by MOE and OCT, and again the teaching portion would be accredited by OCT. Given the ongoing message that government would not fund graduate programs in teacher education, this news was surprising. There was a reaction. In particular, I note the article titled *Rivals Rip over Masters Plan for Would Be Teachers* published in the *Star* on May 6th 2014.

Issues raised have been lack of transparency, MTCU funding, purview, and the MTCU differentiation agenda which emerged at the time of writing in an article in *University Affairs* (MacDonald, 2014), titled *OISE Explains Its Decision to Drop BEd Programs*. MacDonald states:

> [the] Ontario government has approved OISE's plan to convert its existing 1,167 BEd spaces into up to 500 additional spaces for two existing graduate degrees—the master of teaching and master of arts in child study and education. The two programs already admit about 200 students annually. OISE anticipates their enrolment will grow to between 430 and 460 admissions. These two graduate-degree programs are just five semesters in all and are unique in the province for preparing students to be teachers within a research-steeped graduate program .... The change at OISE takes effect just as the Ontario government is requiring all undergraduate teacher education programs to increase to four semesters from two semesters currently. In addition, other Ontario universities' teaching faculties face a mandated 50-percent cut to their annual undergraduate admissions—a government response to a glut of unemployed BEd graduates who can't find work in their preferred profession. The faculties also face a 33-percent cut in government funding for the BEd spaces remaining. (MacDonald, 2014)

The practicalities of the funding difference are that the 3.0 BIU weight for the OISE M. Teaching masters student translates into $13,205 per student, which compares unfavorably with the 1.5 BIU weight at $5,684 for a B.Ed student at all the other faculties of education in Ontario.

Significantly, the dean at OISE UT cites, as a rationale for the M. Teaching, the MTCU differentiation agenda. Citing the dean, MacDonald (2014) writes: "We wanted to be sure that whatever we did allowed us to make our unique contribution to the teaching profession ... and it is our graduate programs, and our research intensity there, that will allow us to do that." MacDonald continues, stating that this is "a response to the government's—and her university's—call for 'differentiation,' where universities are encouraged to focus on their unique program strengths instead of trying to be all things to all students" (MacDonald, 2014). The U of T news release said the move "plays to the strengths of the University of Toronto as an advanced research institution responding to the needs of a diverse population and a changing economy" (University of Toronto, 2014).

At the time of writing, the Ontario provincial election is imminent. If the story unfolds as I anticipate it will, teacher education in Ontario may indeed follow MTCUs differentiation agenda. In the interim, the Brock PCA, along with others submitted in Fall 2013, have not yet been approved by MTCU. I expect we must wait for the new government to judge both the PCAs and SMAs. Meantime, I am certain internal discussions are taking place at all the other 12 publically funded universities in Ontario. At Brock we are open to change and to renewing our vision of and for teacher education and graduate studies in education. And as we do so, I am reminded of the great art historian Linda Nochlin's (1988) thesis, "the personal is political" (p. 146). Indeed.

NOTES

[1] The 13 universities are Lakehead University; Laurentian University (French and English); Nipissing University; York University; Queens University; Trent University; The University of the Ontario Institute for Technology; OISE/University of Toronto; Wilfred Laurier University, Brock University, Western University and the University of Windsor and Ottawa University.

REFERENCES

Alfonso, C., Morrow, A., & Bradshaw, J. (2013, June 5). Ontario moves to halve number of teachers-college grads. The *Globe and Mail*. Retrieved from http://www.theglobeandmail.com/news/national/ontario-moves-to-halve-number-of-teachers-college-grads/article12357404/

Association of Canadian Deans of Education. (2005). *Accord on initial teacher education*. Retrieved from http://www.csse-scee.ca/acde/accords

MacDonald, M. (2014, June 4). OISE explains its decision to drop B.Ed programs. *University Affairs*. Retrieved from http://www.universityaffairs.ca/OISE-explains-its-decision-to-drop-BEd-programs.aspx

Moodie, G. (2013, September 4). How to differentiate universities. *University Affairs*. Retrieved from http://www.universityaffairs.ca/how-to-differentiate-universities.aspx

Nochlin, L. (1988). Why have there been no great women artists? In L. Nochlin (Ed.), *Women, art and power and other essays* (pp. 144-178). New York, NY: Harper and Row.

Ontario College of Teachers Act. (1996a). Retrieved from http://www.e-laws.gov.on.ca/html/regs/english/elaws_regs_020347_e.htm

Ontario College of Teachers Act. (1996b). *Accreditation of teacher education program.* Retrieved from http://www.e-laws.gov.on.ca/html/source/regs/english/2013/elaws_src_regs_r13283_e.htm

Toronto Star, The. (2014, May 6). Rivals rip U of T over master's plan for would-be teachers. *The Toronto Star.* Retrieved from http://www.thestar.com/yourtoronto/education/2014/05/06/rivals_rip_u_of_t_over_masters_plan_for_wouldbe_teachers.html

University of Toronto News Release. (2014, May 2). *U of T master's programs enhance quality of teaching in Ontario.* Retrieved from http://www.oise.utoronto.ca/oise/About_OISE/Realignment_of_Teacher_and_Graduate_Education_at_OISE/News_Release.html

Weingarten, H., & Deller, F. (2010) *The benefits of greater differentiation in Ontario's universities sector.* Final report. The Higher Education Quality Council of Ontario. Retrieved from http://www.heqco.ca/siteCollectionDocuments/DifferentiationENG.pdf

Fiona Blaikie
Dean and Professor
Faculty of Education
Brock University
Ontario, Canada

LAURENT CAMMARATA, MARTINE CAVANAGH &
YVETTE D'ENTREMONT

3. LA RESTRUCTURATION DU PROGRAMME EN ÉDUCATION AU CAMPUS SAINT-JEAN DE L'UNIVERSITÉ DE L'ALBERTA

L'Importance du Rôle des Leaders du Milieu Académique

INTRODUCTION

Le monde est changeant et les programmes de formation des enseignants doivent constamment se renouveler afin de pouvoir mieux répondre aux besoins des futurs enseignants qui auront à faire face à un monde éducatif de plus en plus complexe. Le programme de formation des enseignants au Campus Saint-Jean (CSJ) a récemment initié une refonte majeure visant à apporter les modifications nécessaires pour mieux répondre aux besoins des futurs enseignants qui se préparent à œuvrer dans un contexte linguistique minoritaire complexe imposant des défis très particuliers. Dans cet article, après avoir décrit le contexte dans lequel nous nous trouvons et certains des défis spécifiques à ce contexte, nous présenterons quelques éléments de solutions ainsi que le processus qui a permis à toute une équipe de travailler ensemble afin de bâtir de nouvelles fondations. En conclusion, nous argumentons que le soutien des leaders du milieu académique est essentiel au succès d'un projet tel que celui dans cet article.

LE CONTEXTE DANS LEQUEL SE SITUE NOTRE PROGRAMME DE FORMATION DES ENSEIGNANTS

Contexte général

L'Alberta est une province majoritairement anglophone avec une présence francophone qui remonte à la fin du 19e et au début du 20e siècle. Celle-ci a été stimulée d'abord par le commerce de la traite des fourrures et ensuite par la colonisation des Canadiens français provenant du Québec et des États-Unis. Des statistiques récentes indiquent qu'aujourd'hui, la province compte environ 80 000 personnes qui ont le français comme première langue officielle parlée (PLOP), seule ou avec l'anglais et que ce groupe comprend environ 17 000 jeunes qui parlent français régulièrement à la maison (Bisson, 2013).

Il existe dans ce contexte des programmes d'éducation en français adaptés aux besoins de ces deux populations: les programmes d'immersion qui comptent presque 37 000 élèves répartis dans 216 écoles (Canadian Parents for French,

2011/2012) et les écoles francophones qui comprennent 6700 élèves répartis dans 34 écoles (Association Canadienne d'Éducation de Langue Française, 2011/2012). En ce qui concerne les programmes d'immersion destinés à la majorité anglophone que l'on retrouve aujourd'hui à travers tout le Canada et qui bénéficient d'une popularité croissante, leur origine est associée à ce qui est maintenant communément appelé l'expérience Saint-Lambert (Lambert & Tucker, 1972) au milieu des années 60, une initiative qui a vu le jour grâce à des parents anglophones vivant à Québec et voulant offrir à leurs enfants une meilleure éducation en français (Roy, 2009). Ces programmes développés pour les apprenants de langue majoritaire, les anglophones dans le contexte de l'Alberta, ont pour but premier le développement du bilinguisme additif, de la bilittératie ainsi que des habiletés académiques et de la compréhension interculturelle chez les apprenants (Tedick & Cammarata, 2012). Parallèlement, on trouve aussi des programmes pour les minorités francophones. Ces programmes ont pu être mis en place grâce à l'adoption en 1982 de l'article 23 de la *Charte canadienne des droits et libertés*, qui donne aux minorités culturelles et linguistiques le droit à l'éducation dans leur langue maternelle à condition que celle-ci fasse partie des deux langues officielles. Il est aussi important de noter que les effectifs dans ces deux contextes ne cessent de croitre.

La formation des enseignants au Campus Saint-Jean: Un programme pas comme les autres

La situation démographique ainsi que le contexte linguistique particulier de l'Alberta tels que décrits ci-dessus expliquent les besoins en matière d'éducation en français et l'importance d'un centre de formation des enseignants tel que celui du CSJ, une des deux seules institutions dans l'ouest canadien avec Saint Boniface à offrir un programme de formation des enseignants complètement en français.

L'histoire du Campus Saint-Jean remonte à l'origine de la présence francophone en Alberta. Fondé par les pères Oblats au début du 20e siècle, à l'origine une école secondaire pour garçons, le campus deviendra un collège en 1950 et sera finalement intégré à l'Université de l'Alberta en 1976 (Levasseur-Ouimet, 1997). Aujourd'hui, cette institution offre aux 630 étudiants qui la fréquentent un environnement entièrement francophone au sein d'une communauté francophone vibrante. Si ces étudiants sont réparties dans 9 programmes différents, il est important de souligner qu'environ 70% d'entre eux se retrouvent dans le programme de formation des enseignants et qu'ils constituent une communauté d'apprenants linguistiquement et culturellement très hétérogène. En effet, 65% des étudiants sont anglophones et ont été scolarisés dans les écoles d'immersion française et le reste, issu pour la plupart des écoles francophones, comprend des étudiants franco-albertains et internationaux.

Ce qui distingue le programme de formation du CSJ des autres programmes accessibles en Alberta, c'est son contexte d'apprentissage unique qui découle de la combinaison de trois caractéristiques: 1) une communauté d'apprenants à taille humaine facilitant des rapports privilégiés entre étudiants et professeurs, 2) une expérience d'apprentissage et de vie universitaire entièrement en français et 3) une préparation visant à outiller les futurs enseignants pour qu'ils soient en mesure d'enseigner efficacement dans deux milieux éducatifs distincts, à savoir les écoles d'immersion et les écoles francophones.

LES DÉFIS MAJEURS AUXQUELS NOUS FAISONS FACE ET NOTRE DÉBUT DE RÉPONSE À CES DÉFIS

Défis majeurs

Le contexte ainsi que les caractéristiques uniques du campus présentent quatre défis particuliers pour la formation des enseignants pour lesquels nous avons tenté de trouver des éléments de solution. Ces quatre défis peuvent être regroupés dans deux catégories distinctes: Les défis de type intrinsèques aux étudiants et les défis extrinsèques.

Les défis intrinsèques aux étudiants touchent à leur capacité à être des modèles langagiers et à s'intégrer harmonieusement dans les communautés éducatives dans lesquels ils seront appelés à œuvrer, un objectif particulièrement difficile à atteindre pour les étudiants internationaux issus de modèles éducatifs souvent très différents. Concernant la compétence en français de nos futurs enseignants dont la majorité a reçu une éducation dans les programmes immersifs, il est important de noter que, malgré le fait que ces étudiants possèdent de bonnes capacités langagières en compréhension orale et écrite, ils ont néanmoins de sérieuses lacunes en production orale et écrite dans les domaines suivants: complexité et précision de la syntaxe et de la grammaire, richesse lexicale et utilisation de langue dans un contexte sociolinguistique approprié (par ex., Harley, 1992; Harley, Cummins, Swain, & Allen, 1990; Mougeon, Nadasdi, & Rehner, 2010). Ces lacunes représentent une barrière importante dans la capacité de ces futurs enseignants à être des modèles linguistiques dans salle de classe et peuvent aller jusqu'à nuire au développement langagier de leurs élèves.

Les défis extrinsèques aux étudiants relèvent de leur formation pédagogique associée aux besoins spécifiques des contextes éducatifs dans lesquels ils vont opérer et sont en rapport avec leur compréhension des particularités propres à ces deux milieux éducatifs distincts. Il est important de noter que la formation pédagogique dont ils ont besoin pour évoluer efficacement dans le contexte immersif exige une capacité à pouvoir intégrer de manière optimale l'enseignement de la langue à tous les contenus disciplinaires tels que les sciences et les études sociales, une nécessité qui a été identifiée clairement par la recherche (Tedick & Cammarata, 2012). De nos jours ce type de formation est aussi pertinent pour œuvrer dans les écoles francophones dont la population est linguistiquement très hétérogène. Cette formation pédagogique implique également que les futurs enseignants soient capables de bien distinguer les missions respectives des deux contextes éducatifs ciblés: dans le cas des écoles francophones, la promotion de la langue et de la culture francophone est un but en soi (mission proche de la revitalisation linguistique et culturelle).

Des éléments de solution pour relever ces défis

Ce qui suit tente de décrire brièvement et de manière générale les interventions mises en place pour répondre aux défis identifiés précédemment. Ainsi, dans un premier temps, nous avons élaboré un référentiel de 12 compétences professionnelles (voir tableau 1) afin de clarifier pour les futurs enseignants les objectifs d'apprentissage visés. Parmi ces douze compétences, quatre d'entre elles ciblent de manière très spécifiques les problématiques identifiées ci-dessus: la

Tableau 1. Référentiel de compétences professionnelles ciblées dans le cadre du programme de formation des enseignants au Campus Saint-Jean

APPRENTISSAGE	CONTEXTE ÉDUCATIF
Développement et apprentissage de l'élève	Effets du contexte sur apprentissage et enseignement
C1: Le futur enseignant comprend la façon dont l'élève se développe et la manière dont il construit ses connaissances.	C8: Le futur enseignant tient compte des effets des variables contextuelles sur l'apprentissage et l'enseignement.
Différences individuelles	Rôle de l'éducateur en contexte d'immersion française et en contexte francophone minoritaire
C2: Le futur enseignant comprend les effets de la diversité sur l'apprentissage de l'élève.	C9: Le futur enseignant adopte un rôle approprié en fonction du contexte éducatif dans lequel il se trouve.
ENSEIGNEMENT	PROFESSIONNALISME
Langue d'enseignement	Réflexion et croissance professionnelle
C3: Le futur enseignant maîtrise la langue française tant à l'oral qu'à l'écrit et communique clairement dans cette langue dans une variété de contextes.	C10: Le futur enseignant adopte une pratique réflexive afin d'optimiser son enseignement et d'orienter son développement professionnel.
Matière	Comportement professionnel et éthique
C4: Le futur enseignant maitrise les concepts, le langage et les formes de littératie propres à la matière enseignée et favorise le développement de la littératie disciplinaire chez l'élève.	C11: Le futur enseignant est un modèle d'éthique démontrant un sens de responsabilité exemplaire vis à vis de sa formation et de la profession enseignante en général.
Évaluation	C12: Le futur enseignant communique efficacement dans les deux langues officielles afin de développer des relations positives avec les divers intervenants du milieu scolaire.
C5: Le futur enseignant reconnaît l'importance de l'évaluation pour guider sa pratique et utilise des méthodes d'évaluation variées et appropriées.	
Planification et stratégies d'enseignement	
C6: Le futur enseignant planifie et enseigne en utilisant des stratégies efficaces pour engager tous les élèves dans leur apprentissage.	
Gestion de classe	
C7: Le futur enseignant a recours à des stratégies de gestion efficaces pour promouvoir un environnement propice à l'apprentissage.	

compétence liée au niveau langagier des étudiants (C3); les compétences liées aux deux contextes éducatifs (C8 et C9) et la compétence associée à l'intégration de la langue et du contenu (C4).

De plus, nous avons mis en place un ensemble de mesures très concrètes afin non seulement de permettre le développement de ces compétences, mais aussi de répondre au défi de l'intégration réussie des étudiants internationaux au système éducatif albertain. Pour permettre le développement de la compétence langagière (C3) nous avons pris trois mesures principales. La première a pris la forme d'un test linguistique sanctionnant l'admission aux stages d'enseignement pratique. Le niveau exigé pour réussir ce test représente, selon le Cadre Européen de Références pour les Langues (CECRL), le niveau supérieur dans la capacité d'utiliser la langue courante dans des contextes variés. La deuxième mesure, a consisté en une refonte des cours de français qui s'est traduite par une progression à double voies: nous avons tout d'abord rehaussé le seuil de la note de passage pour passer au cours suivant et inclut des cours de consolidation pour ceux n'ayant pas réussi à atteindre ce seuil. La troisième mesure a consisté à inclure dans tous les travaux exigés dans les cours en éducation une note sanctionnant la qualité de la langue écrite. Pour les compétences liées aux contextes éducatifs (C8 et C9), nous avons mis en place un système de laboratoire permettant aux étudiants, dès le début de leur formation et tout au long de celle-ci, de mettre en pratique leurs savoirs théoriques dans des milieux scolaires culturellement très variés. Afin de répondre à la compétence portant sur l'intégration de la langue et du contenu (C4), nous avons créé un nouveau cours pour préparer les futurs enseignants à utiliser une approche de développement de programme et d'enseignement spécifiquement adaptée. Parallèlement, nous avons intégré la dimension littératie académique à tous les cours de didactique des matières.

CONCLUSION: UN PROCESSUS DE REFONTE QUI NE PEUT SE FAIRE EN ISOLATION

Ce qui a rendu ce projet de renouveau possible et son exécution rapide et efficace, nous en sommes convaincus, est le fait que celui-ci a été bâti sur l'idée que seul un processus démocratique pouvait amené une équipe aussi large que la nôtre (15 membres) à construire quelque chose de solide et durable. Durant une année entière, nous nous sommes réunis très fréquemment et avons travaillé tous ensemble pour définir une nouvelle vision pour notre programme, une fondation sur laquelle nous avons pu ensuite construire. Nous avons aussi collaboré pour identifier les défis majeurs auxquels le travail de refonte se devait de répondre. Cet exercice nous a permis de développer un cadre de référence reflétant notre vision globale de ce à quoi devait ressembler notre programme dans les années à venir. Toutes les décisions importantes concernant le programme ont été le fruit de discussions souvent animées où nous avons cherché à trouver un consensus afin que tous les membres de notre famille académique puissent participer activement à ce grand projet éducatif. De plus, il faut noter que toutes les décisions importantes ont été prises à l'unanimité renforçant ainsi la capacité de tous à s'approprier, en quelque sorte, le nouveau programme.

Nous concluons notre réflexion en argumentant que tout changement de cette envergure ne peut être fait en isolation et qu'il nécessite une collaboration étroite avec les membres proéminents de l'administration ainsi qu'un soutien adéquat au niveau des ressources financières et humaines. Il y a tant de travail à faire pour mettre en place un nouveau programme ou un programme réformé de manière significative comme le nôtre, que cela ne peut pas être accompli si les ressources humaines et financières ne sont pas au rendez-vous et si la vision d'une équipe telle que la nôtre n'est pas entièrement partagée par tous les membres y compris et surtout ceux de la haute administration. Ceci nous amène à souligner le rôle capital de la haute direction (doyen et vice-doyens) dans l'aboutissement de projet de restructuration tel que celui décrit dans cet article, une restructuration impossible à mener à bien sans leurs propres croyances dans le bien-fondé et l'importance de la mission à accomplir.

RÉFÉRENCES

Association Canadienne d'Éducation de Langue Française/ACELF (2011-2012). *Outils d'intervention: Carte des écoles francophones*. Repéré à http://www.acelf.ca/outils-pedagogiques/carte-ecoles-francophones.php

Bisson et Associé.e.s Inc. (2013). *Document de consultation-semaine du 17 février 2013* Rapport. Ottawa, ON: Author.

Canadian Parents for French/CPF (2011-2012). *Media Quick facts*. Repéré à http://www.cpfalta.ab.ca/Media/quickfacts.htm

Harley, B. (1992). Patterns of second language development in French immersion. *Journal of French Language Studies, 2*, 159-183.

Harley, B., Cummins, J., Swain, M., & Allen, P. (1990). The nature of language proficiency. In B. Harley, P. Allen, J. Cummins, & M. Swain (Eds.), *The development of second language proficiency* (pp. 7-25). Cambridge, UK: Cambridge University Press.

Lambert, W. E., & Tucker, G. R. (1972). *The bilingual education of children: The St. Lambert experiment*. Rowley, MA: Newbury House.

Levasseur-Ouimet, F. (1997). *Regards, paroles et gestes: en souvenir du 20e anniversaire de la Faculté Saint-Jean*. Edmonton: University of Alberta.

Mougeon, R., Nadasdi, T., & Rehner, K. (2010). *The sociolinguistic competence of immersion students*. Bristol, UK: Multilingual Matters.

Roy, S. (2009). Enseigner et apprendre le français en Alberta. *Education Canada, 49*(1), 8-12.

Tedick, D. J., & Cammarata, L. (2012). Content and language integration in K-12 contexts: Student outcomes, teacher practices, and stakeholder perspectives. *Foreign Language Annals, 45*(s1), s28-s53.

Laurent Cammarata
Martine Cavanagh
Yvette d'Entremont
Campus Saint-Jean
University of Alberta
Alberta, Canada

LAURENT CAMMARATA, MARTINE CAVANAGH &
YVETTE D'ENTREMONT

3A. RESTRUCTURING THE TEACHER EDUCATION PROGRAM AT THE CAMPUS SAINT-JEAN OF THE UNIVERSITY OF ALBERTA

The Importance of Academic Leaders

INTRODUCTION

The world is changing and teacher-training programs must be constantly renewed to meet the needs of future teachers who will have to face an educational situation that is increasingly complex. The Education Program at the Campus Saint-Jean (CSJ), a four-year baccalaureate program designed primarily to prepare students to teach in French-immersion and French first-language (or "Francophone") schools, has recently undergone a major restructuring involving necessary changes to better meet the needs of future teachers who will work in complex linguistic-minority contexts that pose several unique challenges. In this essay, after a brief description of our situation and some of the specific concerns that it entails, we present some elements of a solution as well as the process that has allowed our team to work together to lay new foundations. In conclusion, we argue that the support of academic leaders is crucial for the success of a project such as this.

THE CONTEXT OF OUR TEACHER-TRAINING PROGRAM

General Context

Alberta is a province with an English-speaking majority and a French-speaking community whose earliest roots date back to the time of the fur trade, but which has grown appreciably since the arrival of French-Canadian settlers from Quebec and the United States at the end of the 19th century. According to the most recent statistics, there are currently approximately 80,000 Albertans whose first official language spoken (or FOLS) is either French or French and English, and this group includes approximately 17,000 children who regularly speak French at home (Bisson, 2013).

The province has two different kinds of French-language programs: French immersion programs serving 37,000 students in 216 schools (Canadian Parents for French, 2011/2012) and 34 Francophone schools with an enrollment of 6,700 students (Association canadienne d'éducation de langue française, 2011/2012). The immersion programs for the English-speaking majority population, which can increasingly be found across Canada, originated with what is commonly referred to as the Saint-Lambert Experiment (Lambert & Tucker, 1972), an experiment launched in the mid 1960s by English-speaking parents in Quebec seeking better French-language education for their children (Roy, 2009). These programs developed for students of the majority-language community, who in the Alberta context are English-speaking, aim at developing learners' additive bilingualism, biliteracy, academic skills and intercultural understanding (Tedick & Cammarata, 2012). Along with these immersion schools for the Anglophone majority, there are now programs for French-speaking minority populations. These programs have been established in accordance with Article 23 of 1982's *Canadian Charter of Rights and Freedoms* which gives cultural and linguistic minorities the right to education in their maternal official language. It is important to note that enrolments in both of these two kinds of programs have consistently grown.

Teacher Education at Campus Saint-Jean: A Program Unlike the Others

Alberta's above-mentioned demographic situation and specific linguistic context explain the French-language needs in education and the importance of having a teacher-training centre such as the CSJ, the only institution in Western Canada besides Winnipeg's Saint Boniface University that offers teacher training entirely in French.

The history of the CSJ goes back to the earliest days of Alberta's French-speaking community. Founded originally as a boys' secondary school by the Oblate Fathers at the beginning of the 20th century, the Campus became a college in 1950 and then was incorporated into the University of Alberta in 1976 (Levasseur-Ouimet, 1997). Today, this institution, which comprises the only Francophone university campus west of Manitoba, offers its 630 students an entirely Francophone environment where it is possible to study, live and socialize in French in an active Francophone and Francophile community. The neighbourhood in which it is situated, called Bonnie Doon, could be described as the epicentre of the Franco-Albertan community: a part of the city of Edmonton with a long Francophone history boasting a French-language clinic and retirement home for the region's Francophones, as well as a commercial centre offering bookstore, restaurant and other services in French.

CSJ's students can choose from one of nine different programs, but approximately 70% of them are registered in the teacher education program where they constitute a linguistically and culturally extremely heterogeneous learning community. The linguistic and cultural makeup of the community can be described as follows: 65% of students are Anglophone who learned French in immersion schools and the rest, coming mostly from Francophone schools, are either Franco-Albertan or of international origin.

What distinguishes CSJ's teacher education program from the others available in Alberta is its unique learning environment characterized by three main facts: 1) its learning community's human scale that promotes enhanced student-professor relationships, 2) the learning experience and university life entirely in French, and

3) the type of teacher preparation it offers that equips students to teach effectively in two distinct environments, namely immersion and Francophone schools.

OUR PRINCIPLE CHALLENGES AND INITIAL RESPONSE

Major Challenges

The CSJ's unique context and characteristics create four particular challenges in terms of teacher preparation, which we have attempted to meet. These four challenges are of two sorts, either intrinsic or extrinsic to our students.

Those challenges that are intrinsic to our students have to do with their ability to be linguistic models and to integrate harmoniously into the educational communities where they will work, the latter task being particularly difficult for some international students who have very different educational backgrounds. As for our future teachers' competence in French, many of those educated in immersion programs, while they possess good abilities in oral and written comprehension, still have rather serious oral and written production deficiencies in the following areas: syntactic and grammatical complexity and precision, lexical resources and the ability to use the appropriate level of language in a variety of sociolinguistic contexts (e.g., Harley, 1992; Harley, Cummins, Swain, & Allen, 1990; Mougeon, Nadasdi, & Rehner, 2010). Consistent with findings from the research literature pertinent to the field (for a synthesis see: Cammarata & Tedick, 2012), these gaps constitute a significant obstacle to these future teachers whose responsibility is to become linguistic models in the classroom, and can even have a negative effect on their students' linguistic development.

The extrinsic challenges have to do with the relationship between our students' pedagogical preparation for meeting the specific needs typically found in the educational contexts in which they will be working, and their understandings of these needs. It is important to keep in mind that being prepared to function effectively in the immersion context requires developing the ability to integrate language teaching into all subjects, be it science or social studies, a requirement which has been clearly identified by research (Tedick & Cammarata, 2012). A similar ability is useful for teachers in Francophone schools where, from a linguistic standpoint, the student population is extremely heterogeneous. At the same time, the necessary teacher preparation must enable our future teachers to distinguish between the respective missions of the two target educational contexts, insofar as one of the Francophone schools' explicit objectives is the promotion of French language and culture (for linguistic and cultural revitalization).

Elements of a Response to These Challenges

The following is an attempt to describe briefly and generally the initiatives we have taken to respond to the challenges mentioned above. First, we developed a list of 12 professional competencies (Table 1) in order to clarify learning goals for the benefit of our future teachers. Of these 12 competencies, four have to do specifically with the above-mentioned challenges: improving our students' linguistic ability (C3), ensuring their acquisition of the abilities appropriate to the two different educational contexts (C8 and C9), and developing their capacity for blending the teaching of language and content (C4).

Table 1. *Analytical List of the Professional Abilities Targeted by the Campus Saint-Jean's Teacher Training Program*

LEARNING	EDUCATIONAL CONTEXT
Student Learning and Development	Effects of Context on Learning and Teaching
C1: The future teacher understands how students develop and build understandings.	C8: The future teacher is conscious of the effects of contextual variables on learning and teaching.
Individual Differences	Educator's Role in French Immersion and Minority Francophone Contexts
C2: The future teacher understands the effects of diversity on student learning.	C9: The future teacher plays an appropriate role according to the educational context.
TEACHING	PROFESSIONALISM
Language of Instruction	Reflection and Professional Growth
C3: The future teacher masters oral and written French and communicates clearly in this language in a variety of contexts.	C10: The future teacher adopts a reflective practice to optimize teaching and guide professional development.
Content	Professional and Ethical Conduct
C4: The future teacher masters the concepts, vocabulary and forms of literacy specific to the subject being taught and promotes the development of student literacy in this area.	C11: The future teacher is an ethical model demonstrating an exemplary sense of responsibility towards professional training and the teaching profession in general.
Assessment	C12: The future teacher communicates effectively in both official languages to develop positive relationships with the various stakeholders in education.
C5: The future teacher recognizes the importance of assessment in guiding teaching practice and uses varied and appropriate means of evaluation.	
Planning and Teaching Strategies	
C6: The future teacher plans and teaches using effective strategies to engage all students in their learning.	
Classroom Management	
C7: The future teacher uses effective management strategies to promote an environment conducive to learning.	

In addition, a set of very concrete measures was put in place not only for the development of competencies, but also to respond to the challenge of successfully integrating international students into Alberta's educational system. Of all the challenges CSJ has sought to meet in revising its teacher education program, supporting the development of future teachers' linguistic competence was without doubt the most difficult. To ensure the development of this competence (C3), we took three main measures. First, we instituted a language test giving admission to student teaching practicums. The level required on this test is, according to the Common European Framework of Reference for Languages (CEFR), the advanced level of the ability to use common language in various contexts. Second, we reorganized our French language courses into a two-track progression by raising the grade required for advancing to the subsequent course and adding a series of parallel consolidation courses for students who do not meet the standard at any given step. Third, we added a mark for the quality of French to all assignments completed by students in our education courses. It should be noted that none of these solutions that we judged to be potentially beneficial was easy to put in place. For one thing, changing the way the program manages future teachers' language development difficulties imposed a very considerable burden of coordination involving two different sections (Art and Languages, responsible for French courses, and Education, in charge of teacher training) whose members do not always share the same beliefs regarding the best way to teach language. A consensus had to be arrived at before going forward. But also, the three measures that we took to raise the level of students' competence in French could have proven prejudicial to both the recruitment and the retention of students, consequences which, in a minority context such as ours, can obviously be of concern to upper-level administration. This is where the support and the sharing of a common vision among the institution's different sections and the dean prove crucial if reforms such as those that we have undertaken are to prove successful.

To address the competencies with regard to educational contexts (C3 and C9), we have put in place a series of laboratories. These labs consist of blocks of schedule time freed up in conjunction with certain courses so that, from the beginning of their training and throughout its duration, students can put their theoretical knowledge into practice in culturally-varied real-school contexts. As for the competence having to do with combining the teaching of language with instruction in different subjects, we have developed a new course that prepares future teachers to use a specifically-adapted approach to preparing appropriate programs and classes. Parallel to this, we have integrated an academic literacy dimension to all subject-specific pedagogy courses.

CONCLUSION: A REORGANIZATIONAL PROCESS THAT CANNOT EXIST IN ISOLATION

We are convinced that what has made this renewal project possible, and ensure an expedited implementation, is our reliance on the idea that only a democratic process could allow a team as large as ours (15 members) to build something strong and durable. For an entire year, all faculty members met frequently and worked all together to come up with a new vision for our program, a foundation on which we were then able to build. We also worked together to identify the principle challenges that this reorganization had to meet. This exercise allowed us to elaborate a frame of reference reflective of our overall vision of what our program should look like in the coming years. All important decisions regarding the program were the result of often animated discussions in which we did our best to come up with a consensus so that all members of our academic family could actively participate in this significant educational project. Furthermore, it is important to note that all important decisions were made unanimously to strengthen each colleague's proprietary interest in the new program.

We conclude our reflection by affirming that no change of this scope can be carried out in isolation, since it requires the close cooperation of the upper levels of administration and sufficient support in the form of financial and human resources. Much work needs to be done to put in place a new or significantly reorganized program like ours, and it cannot be accomplished if the necessary financial and human resources are lacking and if the vision of a team such as ours is not completely shared by all staff members, including and especially those in upper-level administration. For this reason, we must emphasize the key role of administrative leaders (deans and vice-deans) in the achievement of restructuring goals like the ones described in this article, for such goals cannot be reached without these people's belief in the pertinence and importance of the mission being undertaken.

REFERENCES

Association Canadienne d'Éducation de Langue Française/ACELF. (2011-2012). *Outils d'intervention: Carte des écoles francophones*. Available from http://www.acelf.ca/outils-pedagogiques/carte-ecoles-francophones.php

Bisson et Associé.e.s Inc. (2013). *Document de consultation-semaine du 17 février 2013*. Report. Ottawa, ON: Author.

Canadian Parents for French/CPF (2011-2012). *Media quick facts*. Available from http://www.cpfalta.ab.ca/Media/quickfacts.htm

Harley, B. (1992). Patterns of second language development in French immersion. *Journal of French Language Studies, 2*, 159-183.

Harley, B., Cummins, J., Swain, M., & Allen, P. (1990). The nature of language proficiency. In B. Harley, P. Allen, J. Cummins, & M. Swain (Eds.), *The development of second language proficiency* (pp. 7-25). Cambridge, UK: Cambridge University Press.

Lambert, W. E., & Tucker, G. R. (1972). *The bilingual education of children: The St. Lambert experiment*. Rowley, MA: Newbury House.

Levasseur-Ouimet, F. (1997). *Regards, paroles et gestes: En souvenir du 20e anniversaire de la Faculté Saint-Jean*. Edmonton: University of Alberta.

Mougeon, R., Nadasdi, T., & Rehner, K. (2010). *The sociolinguistic competence of immersion students*. Bristol, UK: Multilingual Matters.

Roy, S. (2009). Enseigner et apprendre le français en Alberta. *Education Canada, 49*(1), 8-12.

Tedick, D. J., & Cammarata, L. (2012). Content and language integration in K-12 contexts: Student outcomes, teacher practices, and stakeholder perspectives. *Foreign Language Annals, 45*(s1), s28-s53.

Laurent Cammarata
Martine Cavanagh
Yvette d'Entremont
Campus Saint-Jean, University of Alberta
Alberta, Canada

HEATHER E. DUNCAN

4. EXPLORING COMPLEXITIES OF LEADERSHIP FOR TEACHER EDUCATION

We live in times of exponential change. Deans of education must play a key role in ensuring teacher education programs provide future teachers the skills to "rethink, unlearn and relearn, change, revise, and adapt" (Niess, 2008, p. 225) so that they may be successful in meeting the diverse needs of the children they will teach. Moreover, leading successful change requires not only awareness of the context of the university as a whole (Bassaw, 2012), but particularly, the organizational culture of the faculty (Thomas, Herring, Redmond, & Smaldino, 2013).

LEADERSHIP FLUX AND ORGANIZATIONAL CULTURE

Change in leadership can be positive and lead to fresh directions; indeed, it is inherent in the typical five-year decanal appointment. However, high levels of leadership turnover may impact organizational cultural negatively. While cross-disciplinary research exists on leadership and turnover, its focus is not on the impact of leadership turnover on the organization and the faculty within in it, but rather on the reasons for leadership attrition (Kippenbrock, 1995; Rosser, 2004) and the influence of leadership style on staff turnover (Clemens, Milsom, & Cashwell, 2009; Galletta, Portoghese, Battistelli, & Leiter, 2013; Green, Miller, & Aarons; 2013; Tremblay, 2010; Wolford, 2012). Some studies in the K-12 educational sector indicate leadership turnover is associated with falling student achievement (Miller, 2013). Given the broader focus and less defined, less measurable, learning outcomes of higher education, it is more difficult to link lack of stability in the dean's position to student success.

Evidence does exist, however, that indicates absence of direction from the dean's office negatively impacts the momentum of the faculty, decreases productivity, and damages the organizational culture (Dulek, 2014). Rapid leadership turnover is associated with lack of shared purpose and cynicism among staff. Continuous change in direction makes it difficult to maintain a focus on innovation and to accomplish meaningful change (Louis et al., 2010). Relationships among faculty members and deans are complex. Trust has been associated with organizational effectiveness (Kramer & Cook, 2004). High levels of trust can positively impact attitudes, behaviours, collaboration, and performance (Costa, 2003). While trust can strengthen ties within a faculty, it is a fragile commodity that is easily damaged, particularly if leadership turnover is fraught with contention, and when hidden agendas and conflicting intentions become overt

(Parse, 2010). When trust is damaged, faculty members may tend to seek safety, to work in isolation, and to concentrate on areas that are beneficial to their own career path rather than on the collective progress of the unit as a whole.

In 2009, Sir Andrew Likierman accepted the position of dean of the London School of Business, the fifth person in that role in eleven years. The Financial Times reported, "Sir Andrew has taken on what might seem like a veritable poisoned chalice" (Bradshaw, 2009, para. 1). On accepting my current position as Dean of the Faculty of Education at a small western Canadian liberal arts university, I became the fifth dean in five years, following failed searches, one-year deans, or acting-deans appointed from within the faculty. Because of financial constraints, several faculty members who retired were not replaced. In addition, a prolonged strike (one of three in recent bargaining history) added to general disenfranchisement among faculty. Although appointed from outside the university, I came with a modicum of inside knowledge in that I had completed a master's degree at the university several years previously. One or two of the faculty from my time as a graduate student remained. I had also been a high school principal in the area and so my style of leadership was known. Thus, in appointing me as dean, the faculty knew a little about who it was getting as dean. However, as I had done my doctoral work elsewhere and been a faculty member at another university for a substantial time period in the interim, I had not experienced the turbulent and somewhat toxic history of the past decade. This was an enormous benefit in the start-up process as my actions and ways of being and doing were not impacted by past experience of a less than positive culture. Starting as dean, I did not feel that I was accepting a "poisoned chalice," although I had been warned prior to accepting the position that challenges lay ahead and that it was my job to provide direction and build trust and engagement among faculty members.

SOCIALIZATION TO ORGANIZATIONAL CULTURE

Organizations are social systems comprising many individuals and groups with widely differing needs and goals. Thus organizations have a human purpose. When an organization fails to meet the goals of those within it, people tend to withdraw from it (Knowles, 1980), as was largely the case in the faculty of which I became dean. Cohesiveness among individual faculty members was fairly high, which was good in that it provided a sense of community. Less than desirable was the lack of trust in administration. My first tasks were to get to know my colleagues, gain an understanding of "how it's done around here," and demonstrate through my actions who I am and how I go about business. As Tremblay (2010) noted, trust takes time to build. However, leaders who are seen as trustworthy by those they lead have a positive impact on staff commitment. Collaboratively setting direction for the future would be the next step.

As a new dean, using my values to guide my interactions with individuals and groups was a key part of becoming socialized to the complexity of campus culture. Before embarking on high-level change, it is important to scan the environment thoroughly and become aware of any hidden obstacles that lurk in the undergrowth.

How open individuals are to change is largely dependent on organizational culture. According to Schein (1992), culture is the "most stable and least malleable" (p.361) part of the organization. Altering the culture of an organization is difficult and so for successful change to occur it must align to some extent with existing culture (Kezar & Eckle, 2002), that is, it must consider the underlying belief systems of those it will impact (Bass, 1985). Deeply held mental models and underlying assumptions (Argyris & Schön, 1978) can trump any change that is incongruent with these. To overcome this challenge requires collaboratively working to redefine organization values while still remaining true to foundational principles and history that faculty may hold dear—changing the shape and capacity of the paradigm rather than replacing it.

MY VISION AS A DEAN OF EDUCATION

The demise of the twentieth century managerial paradigm (Greenfield, 1995) began in K-12 education when the leadership focus shifted towards instructional leadership. In the higher education sector, over the past decade, increasing emphasis is also being put on leadership for learning and teaching (de la Harpe & Mason, 2014). Leading teaching and learning is how I view a major part of my role as dean. To lead for teaching and learning, first one must establish direction; second, communicate it to stakeholders, and third motivate and inspire stakeholders and align resources to meet to go forward (Marshall, Orrell, Cameron, Bosanquet, & Thomas, 2011).

Most pre-service teacher education programs currently are delivered in traditional, face-to-face formats that provide little flexibility for non-traditional learners (Enns & Duncan, 2001). To be relevant in the current societal climate, programs must meet the needs of a different generation of learners. My vision for teacher education is to develop flexible, learner-centred programs that focus on inquiry and experiential approaches to learning. A recent document, *Bringing Life to Learning* (Council of Ontario Universities, 2014), states experiential learning sets students up for success in the workplace. Implementing such an approach may require challenging students to go beyond the traditional cookie-cutter approach to success in the classroom towards becoming reflective practitioners who examine their practice through a critical lens (Enns, 2006). My vision for faculty is that they collaboratively engage in the scholarship of teaching and learning in which they critically examine student learning through the lens of student learning outcomes (Hutchings, Huber, & Ciccone, 2011).

Achieving these two visions will take time. Importantly, perhaps due to the lack of clear direction during the leadership flux within this faculty and also owing to a cumbersome departmental structure that was imposed by higher administration over a decade ago, the majority of faculty members have embraced the first stage of change: restructuring the faculty into departments and committees that will allow for maximum faculty participation in decision-making. One important facilitating element was the degree of choice and autonomy afforded to faculty during the collaborative process of restructuring. Choosing to start innovation in an area in which faculty identified a need, eliminated contention and established a foundation for a shared decision-making structure. Giving faculty voice and choice in the process created ownership. As a result, several key individuals have taken a leadership role. Beginning with a non-threatening change provided a framework of collaborative working norms that will allow us to tackle more difficult issues when they arise.

Schein (1992) commented on the difficulty of changing organizational culture. Dulek (2014) noted the negative impact of leadership turnover on organizational culture: when leadership is lacking people disengage (Knowles, 1980). Thus, instead of changing the organizational culture, the restructuring process may have provided an impetus for the re-emergence of an organizational culture that had lain dormant during years of flux, which may also account for the enthusiasm rather than resistance with which this change was met.

SETTING DIRECTION

The next step forward is program review, a process filled with complexities, as we look toward revisiting degree expectations, program outcomes, and drill down to the key areas that need to be addressed in our programs to prepare future teachers, as well as look to alternative modes of delivery. Faculty have ownership of certain areas of the curricula and establishing priorities may be a challenge. While K-12 curriculum follows strict provincial guidelines, academic freedom is cherished in higher education. However, during the past year we have been engaged in an environmental scan and gained much input regarding important skills needed for success in the classroom by consulting with current students, previous students now teaching in K-12 schools, division superintendents, and principals. We will use these data to further inform our decisions.

My first year as dean of a faculty of education has been challenging at times, but fulfilling: not a cup laced with arsenic but perhaps a strong espresso that keeps me awake some nights. Bassaw (2011) stated that deans should be provided training to prepare them for a position filled with complexities. In smaller universities, it's probably fair to say, such training rarely occurs. I was fortunate to come to the deanship bringing lessons learned from a lifetime in education in both the K-12 and higher education sectors, as a teacher, principal, faculty member, and department head. Faculties of education are complex structures. But they are comprised of people who have vast experiences and knowledge, and who, on the whole, want to do their best as educators. As dean, it is my task to honour the individuals with whom I work, provide avenues to maximize their collective capacities, and challenge them to go beyond the status quo and be responsive to a changing environment. As I continue to work with faculty on our collaborative journey towards building our teacher education programs to prepare teachers who are ready for the challenges of their classrooms, it is vital that I stay true to my values, utilize my strengths and those of my colleagues, collaborate freely, and converse honestly.

REFERENCES

Argyris, C., & Schön, D. A. (1978). *Organizational learning: A theory of action perspective*. Reading, MA: Addison-Wesley.

Bassaw, B. (2012). Determinants of successful deanship. *Medical Teacher, 32*, 1002-1006.

Bradshaw, D. (2009, March 9). Familiar face at the top. *The Financial Times*. Retrieved from http://www.ft.com/cms/s/2/4587e96c-1565-11de-b9a9-0000779fd2ac.html#axzz2xNnzm5rA

Bass, B. (1985). *Leadership and performance beyond expectations*. New York, NY: The Free Press.

Clemens, E. V., Milsom, A., & Cashwell, C. S. (2009). Using leader-member exchange theory to examine principal-school counselor relationships, school counselors' roles, job satisfaction, and turnover intentions. *Professional School Counseling, 13*(2), 75-85.

Costa, A. C. (2003). Work team trust and effectiveness. *Personnel Review, 32*, 605-622.

Council of Ontario Universities. (2014). *Bringing life to learning at Ontario Universities*. Retrieved from http://www.cou.on.ca/publications/reports/pdfs/march262014---experiential-learning-report

de la Harpe, B., & Mason, T. (2014). Leadership of learning and teaching in the creative arts. *Higher Education Research & Development, 33*, 129-143.

Dulek, R. (2014). The search is on. *BizEd, 13*(1), 40-44.

Enns, R. J. (2006). Windshield research. Presentation at Manitoba Education Research Network (MERN) Conference, April 28, 2006, Winnipeg, MB.

Enns, R. J., & Duncan, H. E. (2001). Western Canadian teacher education and development: Context and focus. *Asia Pacific Journal of Teacher Education, 4*, 17-25.

Galletta, M., Portoghese, I., Battistelli, A., & Leiter, M. P. (2013). The roles of unit leadership and nurse-physician collaboration on nursing turnover intention. *Journal of Advanced Nursing, 69*, 1771-1784. doi:10.1111/jan.12039

Green, A., Miller, E., & Aarons, G. (2013). Transformational leadership moderates the relationship between emotional exhaustion and turnover intention among community mental health providers. *Community Mental Health Journal, 49*, 373-379. doi:10.1007/s10597-011-9463-0

Greenfield, W. D. (1995). Toward a theory of school administration: The centrality of leadership. *Education Administration Quarterly, 31*, 60-85.

Hutchings, P., Huber, M., & Ciccone, A. (2011). *The scholarship of teaching and learning reconsidered: Institutional integration and impact*. San Francisco, CA: Jossey-Bass.

Kezar, A., & Eckel, P. D. (2002). The effect of institutional culture on change strategies in higher education: Universal principles or culturally responsive concepts. *Journal of Higher Education, 73*, 4.

Kippenbrock, T. (1995). Turnover of hospital chief nursing officers. *Nursing Economics, 13*, 330-336.

Knowles, M. S. (1980). *The modern practice of adult education: From pedagogy to andragogy*. Englewood Cliffs, NJ: Prentice Hall/Cambridge.

Kramer, R. M., & Cook, K. S. (2004). Trust and distrust in organizations: Dilemmas and approaches. In R. M. Kramer & K. S. Cook (Eds.), *Trust and distrust in organizations: Dilemmas and approaches* (pp. 1-18). New York, NY: Russell Sage.

Louis, K. S., Leithwood, K., Wahlstrom, K. L., Anderson, S. E., Michlin, M., Mascall, B., ... Moore, S. (2010). *Learning from leadership: Investigating the links to improved student learning*. Minneapolis: University of Minnesota Retrieved from http://www.wallacefoundation.org/knowledge-center/school-leadership/key-research/Documents/Investigating-the-Links-to-Improved-Student-Learning.pdf

Marshall, S. J., Orrell, J., Cameron, A., Bosanquet, A., & Thomas, S. (2011). Leading and managing learning and teaching in higher education. *Higher Education Research & Development, 30*(2), 87-103. doi:10.1080/07294360.2010.512631

Miller, A. (2013). Principal turnover and student achievement. *Economics of Education Review*, 3660-3672. doi:10.1016/j.econedurev.2013.05.004

Niess, M. L. (2008). Guiding pre-service teachers in developing TPCK. In AACTE Committee on Innovation and Technology, *Handbook of technological pedagogical content knowledge for educators* (pp. 223-250). New York, NY: Routledge.

Parse, R. R. (2010). Human dignity: A human becoming ethical phenomenon. *Nursing Science Quarterly, 23*, 257-262.

Rosser, S. V. (2004). *The science glass ceiling: Academic women scientists and the struggle to succeed.* New York, NY: Routledge.

Schein, E. H. (1992). *Organizational culture and leadership* (2nd ed.). San Francisco, CA: Jossey-Bass.

Thomas, T., Herring, M., Redmond, P., & Smaldino, S. (2013). Leading change and innovation in teacher preparation: A blueprint for developing TPACK ready teacher candidates. *Techtrends: Linking Research & Practice to Improve Learning, 57*(5), 55-63. doi:10.1007/s11528-013-0692-7

Tremblay, M. A. (2010). Fairness perceptions and trust as mediators on the relationship between leadership style, unit commitment, and turnover intentions of Canadian forces personnel. *Military Psychology, 22*, 510-523. doi:10.1080/08995605.2010.513271

Wolford, S. (2012). Incumbents, successors, and crisis bargaining: Leadership turnover as a commitment problem. *Journal of Peace Research, 49*(4), 517-530. doi:10.1177/0022343312440807.

Heather E. Duncan
Brandon University
Manitoba, Canada

KIMBERLY FRANKLIN

5. REFLECTIONS ON CHANGE LEADERSHIP IN A FAITH BASED TEACHER EDUCATION PROGRAM

Tension arises within me when I think about change leadership. Linking these words too closely implies that leadership is only about change. However, very often and very importantly leadership is about sustaining what is already present and good (Hargreaves & Fink, 2006). I also have concerns about how change is related to the modern myth of progress, as well as how change, even good change, can be the result of an abusive use of power. We often justify violent imposition when change is perceived as right, without remembering that any good imposed has the capacity to become a nightmare (Franklin, 2010). However, I also empathize with the longing for change in teacher education, and education in general, and the necessity for perpetual movement towards the good(s) that are not present in our practice (Britzman, 2003; Huebner, 1999; MacIntyre, 1984; Noddings, 1984; Palmer, 1998).

The gap that exists between all that we long for and love in our practice and our current reality is always present, and at times overwhelming. As educators we carry the suffering of multiple inequities present in schools and communities, the suffering of the increasing complexity of our practice, the suffering of limited resources and competing philosophies and values, and the suffering of our own helplessness in the face of these realities. We enter the profession of teaching because we care about this suffering and long to participate in its transformation through the wholehearted offering of ourselves. We become teacher educators because we are hopeful rather than cynical, and we want to nurture a similar way of being in teacher candidates. The gap must be minded. We should try to see realistically all that we are not, and move towards a vision that is better while sustaining that which is already true, good and beautiful. However, we should also "mind" the way that we are "minding," or be "mindful" about the Spirit that conditions our efforts to transform our practice, or the quality of inner life that accompanies or "clothes" our practice (Franklin, 2010). Change that is democratic, peaceful, lasting and meaningful requires this mindfulness.

MINDING THE GAP WITH HUMILITY

To be humble is to know one's self through becoming aware of what or who one is not. It is to be conscious of our absolute contingency, to know that there is nothing we can do on our own but still much we can offer to others, to see ourselves as part of a story that is greater than any one person or circumstance, to know that the gap will always be there, to let the gap be and find a way to live within the tension of its presence. "To be human seems to mean being in a predicament that one cannot solve" (Butler, 2005, p. 103). This humility serves us by confronting us with our own poverty, the presence of the gap within us, and the many ways we are not who we want to be or could be. Our western, modern culture conditions us to see ourselves as "messiahs" or "agents of change." In contrast, the practice of humility teaches us to see ourselves as responsible to others, subjects in need of change. When we, as educators and leaders, understand our own shortcomings, a tender and gentle heart is cultivated and we offer ourselves less as critical judges imposing often unwise solutions and more as compassionate co-seekers, open to possibilities and new understandings.

This humility also protects us from the dangers of activism, speed and overwork, which Thomas Merton (1966) calls "a pervasive form of contemporary violence to which the idealist ... most easily succumbs." He says that the "frenzy of our activism neutralizes our work for peace" and "destroys the fruitfulness of our work, because it kills the root of inner wisdom" (p. 73). Frenzy, speed and succumbing to the many pressures of progress closes our eyes and our ears, tightens our hearts and clenches our fists, and leads to forcing instead of supporting, demanding instead of inviting (Purkey, 1999; Purkey & Novak, 1996). Humility makes it possible for us to breathe, to receive and appreciate the offerings of others, to do what we can to make room for others. We find we are not alone in our efforts, and that it is okay not to know all. We do the good we know, small offering that it is, trusting that the rest will be revealed to us or those beyond us.

MINDING THE GAP WITH STILLNESS AND ATTENTION

In order to move towards what we love or long for, we must be able to see what is present, as well as what is not present or what is only veiled. We need eyes oriented towards the goodness, truth and beauty that permeate our practice, and invite our participation even in the midst of the darkness that is also present (Franklin, 2012). The only possible way to see what is invisible or hidden is to love stillness more than action, to understand stillness as a precondition to action, or the light that reveals a path. By stillness, I mean the ascetic act of self-emptying, of calming our inner thoughts, of letting go of our own agenda, and of reflecting on the use of our own freedom, in order to care for the freedom of others. This work of attending is important because it slows us down, it embodies us, and makes it impossible for us to do our work in unethical ways.

> Attention, taken to its highest degree, is the same thing as prayer. It presupposes faith and love ... The attention turned with love towards God (or in a lesser degree, towards anything which is truly beautiful) makes certain things impossible for us. Such is the non-acting action of prayer in the soul. There are ways of behaviour which would veil such attention should they be indulged in and which, reciprocally, this attention puts out of the question .... The poet produces the beautiful by fixing his attention on something real. It is the same with the act of love. (Weil, 1986, pp. 212, 214)

This stillness is a struggle. It is so easy to let routines and demands get to us, to forget that our work is done on holy ground because it involves the souls of others. To still ourselves enough to pay attention leads to a sense of reverence for those you are serving as well as growth in patience and gentleness (Buber, 1970). Our looks don't glance in disinterest or bounce off in haste. We are present enough to hold the other in our gaze, to draw out the other, to reach the other with eyes and heart, to take in the other, to call the other. Attention is a gift given to the beloved—we only really attend to who or what we love (Franklin, 2013).

When we see or attend well, we also hear well. We start to care more about hearing voices than having a voice. We stop living our lives as though we were "thrown stones," unaware of those we injure and harm in our personal quests to realize our ideals. We become more careful and intentional, and less fearful. We find ways to build community and harmony in the midst of difficulty and diversity, because people usually give back what they receive. Through our attention and care, arising from stillness, a vision for change is revealed rather than articulated and becomes a shared experience rather than an imposed agenda. True democracy becomes possible when true selves are present.

MINDING THE GAP THROUGH GRATITUDE

Minding gaps that represent significant suffering can be overwhelming and can result in ongoing negative critique about the present and growing cynicism about the future. We can develop a sense of never being enough, never having enough, never achieving enough. Gratitude reorients us, raises us up when we are in despair, and keeps us in the present where fullness can break through. We stop existing in a world that is scarce and begin to see a world that is abundant. Our sorrow is brightened, not ignored or overlooked, but brightened. We find life and offer life with this quality of Spirit. We fight less against the things that we cannot control, and spend more time nurturing what is given to us. Gratitude teaches us the remembrance of the goods, the grace of great things, and this remembrance invites us to respond with reciprocal goodness and generosity (Grudin, 1990).

WHAT THE SPIRIT MAKES POSSIBLE IN A TEACHER EDUCATION PROGRAM

In my work as dean I have experienced patterns of interaction that begin to arise which are recognizably related to humility, stillness, attention and gratitude. Faculty decisions become truly democratic in the sense that lines are not previously drawn prior to a meeting. Participants come with open minds instead of agendas, and a willingness to explore a mystery or question together and then draw tentative lines together. Community life is consistently joyful and encouraging rather than fearful and competitive. Time is taken to be together, to share life together, to celebrate together. There is space for being and breathing, less pressure to perform and do. This space makes is possible for new ideas and thoughts to emerge. Policy is used to attentively interpret situations, not determine outcomes. Change is understood as continuous, dynamic and emergent, illuminated by a horizon of timeless and timely "goods." Vision is co-created and never harshly imposed or rigidly interpreted. Faculty and staff development is invitational and encouraged, not incentivized through a punishment and reward paradigm. There is a refusal to determine paths for individuals. Instead ongoing gratitude is expressed for who they are becoming, what they are already offering. Support is provided for directions that emerge from their own understandings of how and what they can offer. As a faculty, we also carry these conditions with us in our interactions with other colleagues and educational partners.

These qualities of Spirit also impact our interactions with students as professors and curriculum planners. We care deeply about the kind of existence or "being" our students experience within our program, with the understanding that they are a unity of body, mind and spirit. We ask ourselves questions about their well-being and the actions we can take to ensure they have opportunities to respond holistically to curriculum and to the demands of the program. We listen to them carefully through ongoing feedback processes. We create space for stillness within classroom interactions, prompt them to wonder, and ensure they experience beauty, truth and goodness in transformative ways. We use the arts as a way of translating genres and deepening understanding. We discourage hoop jumping and minimalistic responses by offering them a curriculum that always points to the more—what is beyond identified student learning outcomes, what is loved, what is still to be known. We have conversations with them that help them explore what it might mean to develop humility, stillness and gratitude within their own practice, and to care about the kind of existence they are creating for their students. We demonstrate that we are still learning with them. These patterns of interaction are ways we help them become aware of the gap, and to help us mind the gap with qualities of Spirit that give them the capacity to take a step back from the abyss and move towards a horizon of hope—in their own practice and for their future students.

It may seem hopelessly idealistic to devote an entire essay about change in teacher education to just a few of the qualities of spirit that create conditions for change, rather than speak specifically about the necessary changes themselves. But I believe we, as educators and leaders, so often get the cart before the horse, or feel pressured to put the cart before the horse. Our institutions condition us to rely entirely on policies or legislation or top down professional norms, and we are then surprised when no real change occurs (Campbell, 2003; Hansen, 2001). People of power appear to rearrange the world, but people of Spirit actually transform the world. If we truly want peaceful, meaningful, lasting, democratic change, we need to become people of Spirit, who prioritize quality of being over quantity of doing.

REFERENCES

Britzman, D. P. (2003). *Practice makes practice: A critical study of learning to teach.* Albany: State University of New York Press.

Buber, M. (1970). *I and Thou* (W. Kaufmann, Trans.). New York, NY: Touchstone.

Butler, J. (2005). *Giving an account of oneself.* New York, NY: Fordham University Press.

Campbell, E. (2003). *The ethical teacher.* Maidenhead, UK: Open University Press.

Franklin, K. (2010). *The dialogical relationship between spiritual and professional identity in beginning teachers: Context, choices and consequences.* Doctoral dissertation. Retrieved from http://summit.sfu.ca/item/10106

Franklin, K. (2012, January 17). *Opening the door to reverence through stillness* [Blog post]. Retrieved from http://educatingwithreverence.com/2012/01/17/love-stillness-more-than-feeding-the-hungry-or-giving-alms-to-the-poor/

Franklin, K. (2013, February 14). *Beholding the beloved into being* [Blog post]. Retrieved from http://educatingwithreverence.com/2013/02/14/beholding-the-beloved-into-being/

Grudin, R. (1990). *The grace of great things.* New York, NY: Ticknor and Fields.

Hansen, D. (2001). *Exploring the moral heart of teaching: Towards a teacher's creed.* New York: Teacher's College Press.

Hargreaves, A., & Fink, D. (2006). *Sustainable leadership.* San Francisco, CA: Jossey-Bass.

Heubner, D. (1999). *The lure of the transcendent: Collected essays by Dwayne E. Huebner.* Mahway, NJ: Lawrence Erlbaum Associates, Publishers.

MacIntyre, A. (1984). *After virtue* (2nd ed.). Notre Dame, IN: University of Notre Dame Press.

Merton, T. (1966). *Conjectures of a guilty bystander.* New York, NY: Doubleday.

Noddings, N. (1984). *Caring.* Berkeley, CA: University of California Press.

Palmer, P. (1998). *The courage to teach.* San Francisco, CA: Jossey-Bass.

Purkey, W. (1999). *Creating safe schools through invitational education.* ERIC Clearing House, ED435946.

Purkey, W., & Novak, J (1996). *Inviting school success: A self-concept approach to teaching learning, and democratic process* (3rd ed.). Toronto, ON: Wadsworth.

Weil, S. (1951). *Waiting for God.* New York, NY: Harper Collins.

Kimberly Franklin
Faculty of Education
Trinity Western University
Alberta, Canada

ROSETTA KHALIDEEN

6. LEADING IN THE TWENTY-FIRST CENTURY LEARNING ENVIRONMENT

Challenging the Deanship

Today's education landscape is being re-shaped by rapidly developing technologies, innovative teaching and learning practices, demanding accountability and a growing realization that education reform is necessary within a globalized world. The nimbleness of our education system to respond to changes in this fast-paced environment is challenged. Many within the system, including deans of education, would like to devise systematic strategies to affect and effect the changes which are taking place, but their difficulties lie with being entrenched in a heavy-laden bureaucratic system that does not readily respond to change, particularly complex and chaotic change.

Historically, our education system has been organized on an industrial model patterned along the bureaucracy developed by Max Weber, where the intent was to structure work around an hierarchy of authority, clear division of labour, implicit rules and impersonality (Adorno & Horkheimer, 1972; Evans, 1999; Habermas, 1984; Madan, 2014). Developed along the lines of the bureaucracy, traditional schooling used a top-down approach to authority and control and included standardization and specialization. This industrialized model of schooling had at its core, pre-determined curricula and textbooks, the measurement of learning through standardized assessment and the impartial grading of students. The goal of schooling was to maintain the status quo. Conformity was rewarded and divergent thinking discouraged. Students had to fit into the mould designed by the system and those who did not were shunted out. The social and administrative structures within schools were also highly authoritarian. The teacher had knowledge and power over students, and administrators, power over teachers (de Boer & Goedegebuure, 2009). Teachers were allowed little autonomy and their involvement in the work of schools was limited to contributing to the knowledge component of the factory that was efficiently churning out tailor-made students.

Current reform is placing demands on the education system to move away from its traditional system of operation to one that adequately prepares students to successfully live in a globalized world. Paramount among the reform ideas is the shift of education to twenty-first century learning which means rethinking existing practices. Twenty-first century learning is a call to dismantle the traditional norms of schooling and to explore new approaches to teaching and learning. Such innovation necessitates changes to our organizational structures and the radical redesign of our educational spaces. My excitement with twenty-first century learning is that it brings new possibilities around the integration of technologies and multimedia forms of learning into classrooms, and focuses on new, relevant and real-world skills for learners to effectively function in a constant changing world. It sheds light on the critical need for an authentic education, based on curricula immersed in the modern media culture of today's society. Trybus (2013), suggests that our students are digital learners who live in real time and are motivated by schooling which addresses real issues in real time. In this sense, twenty-first century learning is "a dramatic departure from the factory model education of the past. It is abandonment, finally, of textbook-driven, teacher-centred, paper and pencil schooling" (Shaw, 2009, p. 13).

Universities have a key role to play in a twenty-first century learning transformation but, similar to schools, universities have also been founding bureaucracies which continue to grow in their historical formats. The huge growth of the post-secondary education sector has not been matched by the growth of creative organizational structures. Instead, there has been growth in policies, procedures, rules and regulations to support a traditional bureaucracy. There are now over a hundred policies at my own university, and I have counted even more at similar institutions. More bureaucratic-like developments are being imposed from outside the institutions by various stakeholders, one such key stakeholder being the government. I am very cognizant that there are increased government scrutiny and reporting, new by-laws and legislations, stringent financial accountability and inflexible funding guidelines to which universities have to adhere. Universities are responding to the external pressures with more internal bureaucratic organizing, but at the same time, they proclaim recognition for a more authentic education. It therefore begs the question as to how deans of education can transform teacher preparation programs and align them with twenty-first century learning in a controversial and complex educational context.

Deans of education are seen as academic leaders and middle managers in the university's organizational structure and our responsibilities include leading change (Buck, 2014). However, providing leadership within a system of education that has been comfortable, predictable and ordered to one that is new, uncertain and chaotic is no small task for any dean. Gallos (2002), describing her role as a dean of a professional school at a large urban public university says that "The Dean's job is complex, gritty and strenuous. It is filled with complicated problems, questions and requests—most of which are ambiguous and compelling" (p. 174). No different from Gallos, de Boer and Goedegebuure (2009), describe deans as middle managers who have to cope with unclear changing educational demands, competing interests from within and without the university, and the inflexibility of the institution's processes and policies. They note that deans face enormous difficulties in being strategic actors, since they are confronted with too many confusing expectations.

As deans of education, we are tasked with battling the structures that have helped to shape our education, and a social and economic environment that is marching in a different direction. The transformation of education linked to twenty first century learning, emphasizes creativity, innovation, equity, responsibility of learners, teacher autonomy and collaboration instead of competition, rigidity, authoritarianism and mistrust. Although many embrace the twenty-first century learning concepts, there are different interpretations of the meaning and outcome of such an education. A plethora of opinions exists among different groups. Teachers have their own spin on what a twenty-first century learning curriculum should contain and so do teacher preparation programs.

I recently attended a meeting on personalized learning where teachers, parents, community groups and Ministry of Education representatives were present. Parents shared their concerns about the future of their children's education in a climate in which they assume teachers will not be doing what they are paid to do, which is teaching. Some parents felt that the children will be sent off to work on their own on whatever activity held their interest and there would be a lack of necessary teacher supervision. An adamant parent declared, "Teachers are paid to teach and not to allow the kids to learn by themselves, particularly when they are only in grade nine." At the same time a community member interjected with, "But things are changing. Students need different skills today than they needed fifty years ago but we are still in the 1950s mode." The one courageous teacher who later joined the debate noted that, "We are being asked to revamp our curriculum and this is being driven by technology enhanced learning but look around, we don't have the technological resources. On the other hand, some schools that have the money are recreating their learning spaces, but I am not so sure if learning itself has changed. What the schools do is eye catching and maybe it satisfies accountability but who has the real vision for learning?"

The question of a clear vision for education reform is valid. I see a lack of clarity with understanding the twenty-first century education reform taking shape. The Great Schools Partnership (2013), in the Glossary of Education Reform notes that despite the inconsistencies and divergent interpretations of twenty-first century learning, it is clear that skills such as critical thinking, problem solving, creativity, innovation, digital literacy among others will have to drive curriculum and teaching reform. Students have to learn different skills from those taught in the twentieth century to meet the demands of a competitive, knowledge based and technology driven society. Andreotti (2010), acknowledges the existing gap and advocates for a move away from a traditional approach to teaching and learning. She says, "There is a mismatch between 20th century teaching and the needs of the 21st century learners which is foregrounded by access to digital technology" (p. 7).

Twenty-first century education is no doubt a contested terrain but there is agreement that a shift in the conceptualization of knowledge and learning is necessary. Arguments stem more or less from the interpretation of the concept and how it should be applied but Andreotti (2010) believes that an educational shift should not be controversial, since changes rest on three sound arguments: the economic shift from industrialization, the need for innovation and the shift to a knowledge based society driven by technological developments. She sees education's role as the development of a workforce which can operate under changing circumstances and views educators as the actors who will need to adjust their thinking and practice in sync with this new social and economic reality.

These arguments should make it easier for deans of education to lead reform in teacher preparation programs for twenty-first century education. I can candidly disclose that deans are still faced with bureaucratic educational institutions which are resistant to change. Across the education domain, including other programs besides teacher preparation, the move towards twenty-first century learning has become mired in issues of resources, where I am told that continuing to do the familiar is cost effective. Arguments lament the prohibitive costs of technology and curricula changes are viewed as additional faculty workload and an impingement on academic freedom. I have heard personalized learning criticized for misleading students into believing that their new skills will guarantee them employment and I have seen certification policies and guidelines used to discourage innovation and creativity which undergird a twenty-first century learning experience. When changes are not supported and labelled *another thing to do*, it is challenging for deans to lead, manage resources, navigate internal and external politics, collaborate with faculty and ensure program effectiveness.

Wolverton and Gmelch (2002), sum up the frustrations and anxieties deans face on a daily basis to satisfy different stakeholders as, "Deans are puppets on strings being pulled in multiple directions" (p. 111). But, we can still provide the necessary synergistic leadership within a chaotic education context if we remain patient and calm and stay focused on the bigger picture and not lose sight of our vision. As the literature on educational leadership literature suggests, there are no short cuts to implementing and managing educational change (Hargreaves, 2005; Fullan, 2009; Holmes, Clement, & Albright, 2013). One of the strategies that has worked for me is to partner with other deans in my own and other institutions to build collaborative rather than competitive relationships. I recognize that forming alliances takes time but these partnerships create a safe environment in which divergent ideas on education reform can be pursued. As a collective, we can monitor the social, political and economic environment to forecast changes and to appropriately deal with these changes. There is strength in numbers, and I have witnessed the concerted action from a group of deans rather than from an individual has resulted in our voices being heard. Finding ways to engage faculty and leverage their strengths can also build an environment of collegiality, trust and support for change. Faculty's role in implementing change cannot be overstated. My use of distributed leadership, particularly with Department Heads and Chairs, has enabled them as leaders of their program areas to engage in collaborative problem solving and the shared responsibility of charting directions for change. As an education leader, I acknowledge that it is my role to bring both the internal and external community together in the movement for education transformation. There is no doubt in my mind that building a twenty-first learning environment requires the commitment of all.

REFERENCES

Adorno, T., & Horkheimer, M. (1972). *Dialect of enlightenment*. London, UK: Continuum.

Andreotti, V. (2010). Global education in the 21st century: Two different perspectives on the "post"of post-modernism. *Journal of Development Education, 2*(2), 5-22.

Buck, M. (2014). Leadership for the 21st century. *Quest, 66*(2), 137-149.

de Boer, H., & Goedegebuure, L. (2009). The changing nature of the academic deanship. *Leadership, 5*, 347-364.

Evans, G. (1999). *Calling academia to account*. Buckingham, UK: SRHE/Open University Press.

Fullan, M. (2009). Large scale reform comes of age. *Journal of Education Change. 10*, 101-113.

Gallos, J. V. (2002). The dean's squeeze: The myths and realities of academic leadership in the middle. *Academy of Management Learning and Education*, 1, 174-184.

Great Schools Partnership, The. (2013). *Glossary of education reform*. Portland, ME: Author. Retrieved from http://www.greatschoolspartnership.org/resources/glossary-of-education-reform/

Habermas, J. (1984). *The theory of communicative action: Reason and the rationalization of society*. Boston, MA: Beacon Press.

Hargreaves, A. (2005). Leadership succession. *The Educational Forum*, 69, 163-168.

Holmes, K., Clement, J., & Albright, J. (2013). The complex task of leading educational change in schools. *School Leadership and Management, 33*, 270-283.

Madan, A. (2014). Max Weber's critique of the bureaucratization of education. *Contemporary Education Dialogue, 11*, 95-113.

Shaw, A. (2009). Education in the 21st century. *Ethos, 17*(1), 11-17.

Trybus, M. (2013). Preparing for the future of education—Equipping students with 21st century skills: An interview with Dr. Robin Fogarty. *The Delta Kappa Gamma Bulletin, 80*(1), 10-15.

Wolverton, M., & Gmelch, W. (2002). *College deans: Leading from within*. Westport, CT: American Council on Education/Oryx Press.

Rosetta Khalideen
Dean, Faculty of Professional Studies
University of the Fraser Valley
British Columbia, Canada

JANE E. LEWIS

7. TEACHERS WHO LIVE IN GLASS HOUSES SHOULD NOT THROW STONES

A Call for Urgent Reform of University Teacher Education

In his discussion of seven metaphors for leadership transformation, Fuda (2012) identifies fire as number one; "the motivational forces that initiate and sustain transformational efforts; including a burning platform and burning ambition, as well as personal and organizational reasons for change" (p. 7). The metaphor provides an apt lens through which to consider critical issues, research and current ways of thinking about teaching, learning, and pedagogy informing educational leadership at Cape Breton University. The once-stable platform of publicly funded universities in Canada, if not fully aflame, is at the very least smouldering. There is a cry for universities in general, and teacher education programs specifically to respond to a lead-for change agenda. In Nova Scotia there is also an urgency to do this, born of necessity.

The recently released report of the Nova Scotia Commission on Building our Economy, *Now or Never* (2014) pulls no punches. The province teeters on the brink of social and economic disaster. It calls for "game changer strategies and transformational goals." It identifies Nova Scotia's excellent post-secondary system, including 10 universities and well-developed Community College system, as an asset in a province with a transformational agenda. The report further points to the critical importance of the P-12 system to support globally competitive student outcomes, highly developed competencies in math and science and a framework that promotes a culture of entrepreneurship. All this is to be achieved within a shrinking demography; a school-age population 40% smaller than it was 40 years ago that continues to decline.

Teacher education programs of the last generation had standard, highly predictable outcomes. Graduates of programs made their way into the Canadian public school system and spent stable careers in classrooms which, save for a coat of paint if one was lucky, hadn't changed in fifty years. This is no longer the case. Today's pre-service teachers, bear a responsibility unlike that of any previous generation of educators; an expectation they will have the prowess and insight to reinvent the very paradigm of the profession they prepare to enter. Moreover, they will be required to do so, while simultaneously preparing Generation Alpha (those learners born after 2010) (McCrindle, 2010), who will need to grapple with global issues significant enough to determine the continuing viability of the planet. Both the charge and the challenge are daunting.

S.E. Elliott-Johns (ed.), Leadership for Change in Teacher Education, 49–53.
© 2015 Sense Publishers. All rights reserved.

What does this mean for teacher education? Poised at the edge of a perfect storm, as learners around the world connect with one another using hand held devices that defy notions of geography and time and redefine the educational equation, there is no longer debate about if technology, globalization, and altered political, economic and demographic landscapes will alter educational paradigms. The only question is how deep the transformation will be and how fast it will occur. The paradigm shift with respect to how we prepare teachers has been disproportionately modest.

Teachers who live in glass houses should not throw stones. The stark truth of the matter is that despite much rhetoric to the contrary, many teacher education programs tend to preach better than practice when it comes to educational change. It is time universities "walked the walk" and modelled the nature and characteristics of the educational transformation we espouse for others, particularly within the programs in which we prepare teachers. They will after all, need to be masters of many things in their careers; technology-supported learning, globalization in all of its forms, change-leadership and personal and professional reinvention. This cannot be a superficial discussion. The changes required are deeply systemic and cultural; a virtual rethinking of what we do and how we do it. Without it, university-led teacher education runs the risk of becoming irrelevant within a sea-change in education that will occur with or without us.

The good news is, despite the water lapping at our boots, we are not yet too late. Moreover, we are not just positioned to reshape the teacher preparation programs for which we are responsible. Arguably, we may be uniquely positioned to help our colleagues, other teachers within the academy, in other disciplines, rethink the educational models in which they operate too. We are after all, at a time where knowing about learning, might be replacing knowing about "stuff" as a new kind of cool within the Academy.

Peter Senge (2006), an American scientist and director of the Centre for Organizational Learning at the MIT Sloan School of Management, suggests that a core principle in an organization's ability to reinvent itself is becoming a learning organization. A similar perspective is shared by Fullan (2001) who notes "at the most basic level, businesses and schools are similar in that in the knowledge society, they both must become learning organizations or they will fail to survive" (p. xi). Both authors suggest the need for organizations to adopt systems thinking and deliberate, strategic action. Ironically, despite being institutional models established for learning, it cannot be assumed that universities themselves are learning organizations, at least not without deliberate leadership to make them so. That's where the teachers in those glass houses might add particular value.

Within the plethora of literature on the subject of leading educational change (Fuda, 2011; Fullan, 2001, 2002; Kutz, 2008), agreement exists that leadership is complicated, highly-contextual and not broadly understood. Its most basic premise however, is simple. Leadership is about people. As much as we tell ourselves we lead initiatives or growth or change, we don't. We lead people. Or more correctly, we create circumstances in which people will follow. Humans are complex, unpredictable and emotional beings; hence the paradox of leadership.

Kutz (2008) proposes a conceptual model of "contextual intelligence" to describe the "the ability to recognize and diagnose the plethora of contextual factors inherent in an event or circumstance, then intentionally and intuitively adjust behaviour in order to exert influence in that context" (p. 18). In contemporary educational contexts which are multi-faceted, complex and fluid, negotiating change calls for highly developed contextual intelligence. "The contextually intelligent practitioner is knowledgeable about how to do something (i.e., has technical knowledge from formal education and observation), but more importantly is wise enough (based on intuition and experience) to know what to do" (p. 24).

At its core, education, like leadership, is a values-based construct. It betters people and their lives. Facilitation of meaningful and sustainable change in education therefore, needs to be similarly focused on the good of those involved. Fullan (2001) describes some of this as a moral purpose: "acting with the intention of making a positive difference in the lives of people it effects." Although our teacher education programs cannot completely abandon the practice-based skill sets long considered standard for entry-to-practice-in teaching, we nonetheless must "get" the impossibility of equipping anyone for realities not yet invented and teach to mindsets that include a high tolerance for ambiguity and appreciation of the need for a moral compass. Our goal with new teachers then, is to empower them as knowledgeable, inquisitive learners and reflective, moral decision makers, prepared to lead change for themselves and others, on a stage that is becoming increasingly global in nature. It is a conceptual shift from instructional leadership, born of research on effective schooling in the '80s to more recent notions of transformational leadership which focus on the ability of organizations and individuals to innovate (Stewart, 2006).

One recent decision within teacher education programming at Cape Breton University that reflects this trend has been the adoption of UNESCO-informed principles of Education for Sustainability (ESD) as an underpinning for all programs. The Council of Ministers of Education in Canada (2010) have also endorsed this work through the creation of a Pan-Canadian framework that calls for the integration of ESD across all levels of education in Canada. Both a philosophical and conceptual framework, "Education for Sustainable Development entails a reorienting of education to guide and motivate people to become responsible citizens of the planet. It addresses the interrelationships among the environment, the economy and society" (p. 7). ESD challenges us to teach to the bigger picture; sustainability of the planet and the quality of life of its citizens. It is a moral-compass framework with equal relevance to global and regional circumstances. CBU is working on graduate programming in this area; a Masters Degree in Sustainability, Creativity and Innovation and a certificate program in Sustainable Entrepreneurship and Innovation. Both credentials, designed for in-service teachers, will be fully supported by technology and designed for teachers around the globe. It is a place where our intent will be to "walk the walk" with other educators from around the world; a most exciting proposition indeed, for a small university on an island in the North Atlantic!

There is a second piece of the good news for teacher educators; that despite the magnitude of the changes facing us, there has probably never been a time when teaching offered a more exciting career choice for those entering the profession. Educational needs around the world vary greatly and there will be no one-size-fits-all solution for the learners of the world. Furthermore, despite an over-supply of teachers in many Canadian contexts, UNESCO (2014) describes a global teacher shortage that will exceed 6.8 million teachers by 2015. As educational contexts become more global, complex and variable, teaching as a practice will become more valuable.

Of the many internal and external conditions encountered in my work as a dean of education, one stands alone in relative importance with respect to leadership; the ability to establish successful relationships, particularly with others of influence. *Spheres of influence* is nomenclature from the corporate world, but the concept of leveraging relationships to get things done, and thereby increasing one's own ability to influence, has relevance within any organization. It is through relationships that leaders define and expand personal spheres of influence and garner that all-important contextual intelligence previously discussed as essential for success. Relationships are also vital assets in resilience and renewal for both people and organizations. In an era when much lament is levied around factors that can't be controlled, a refreshing and empowering aspect of relationship building is one of self-determination.

Do I have a particular vision about where we need to lead teacher education over the next several decades? On this, I take wise counsel from Peter Senge (2006), who describes himself as a "pragmatic optimist." That is exactly what I believe we need to strive to do in teacher education; to create new educators who are pragmatic optimists; educators who understand principles of leading change, and do so with a moral purpose that will help them find the right place in the end. Over almost three decades as an educational professional I have come to believe that teaching and leadership are inextricably linked; to teach is to lead and to lead is to teach. Amid the turmoil and technology, the foundation of both constructs, remains about people and relationships. That part of teaching has not changed.

Just a decade or two ago, a Canadian teacher worked within a local jurisdiction to help learners connect with information; providing them with new ways of knowing with which to improve their lives. It was a noble calling. In the new order, Canadian teachers can and will work in the global arena to help learners connect with one another and seek collaborative solutions to the complex problems of the world. It is work that still focuses on helping others improve their lives and is still, very much a noble calling.

It was Archimedes who said "Give me a lever long enough ... I shall move the world." How is that for pragmatic optimism? Archimedes is popularly thought to have been a very bright guy. But if he lived in the 21st century he would no doubt have chosen different technology. Any mathematician worth his salt would have to know that if he really wanted to move the world, he should use teachers.

REFERENCES

Council of Ministers of Education, Canada, Education for Sustainable Development Working Group. (2010). *Developing a pan-Canadian ESD framework for collaboration and action: Background paper.* http://cmec.ca/Publications/Lists/Publications/Attachments/222/ESD-collaboration-action.pdf

Fuda, P. (2011). *Leadership transformation: Creating alignment from the inside-out.* Sydney, AUS: The Alignment Partnership. http://www.peterfuda.com/wp-content/themes/peterfuda-bootstrap/content/Leadership-transformation-Creating-alignment-from-the-inside-out_White-Paper.pdf

Fullan, M. G. (2001). *Leading in a culture of change.* San Francisco, CA: Jossey-Bass.

Fullan, M. G. (2002). The change leader. *Educational Leadership, 59*(8), 16-20. Retrieved from http://www.michaelfullan.ca/media/13396052090.pdf

Kutz, M. R. (2008). Toward a conceptual model of contextual intelligence: A transferable leadership construct. *Leadership Review, 8,* 18-31.

McCrindle, M. (2010). *Beyond Z; Meet Generation Alpha. An excerpt from the ABC of XYZ.* Retrieved from http://mccrindle.com.au/resources/whitepapers/McCrindle-Research_ABC-10_Beyond-Z_Meet-Generation-Alpha_Mark-McCrindle.pdf

Nova Scotia Commission on Building our Economy, The. (2014). *Now or never: An urgent call for action for Nova Scotians.* Halifax, NS: Government of Nova Scotia. Senge, P. M. (2006). The fifth discipline: The art and practice of the learning organization. New York, NY: Doubleday.

Stewart, J. (2006). Transformational leadership: An evolving concept examined through the works of Burns, Bass, Avolio and Leithwood. *Canadian Journal of Educational Administration and Policy, 54,* 1-29.

UNESCO. (2014). *Global teacher shortage.* Retrieved from http://www.unesco.org/new/en/education/themes/leading-the-international-agenda/education-for-all/advocacy/global-action-week/gaw-2013/global-teacher-shortage/

Jane E. Lewis
Interim Dean, School of Professional Studies
Associate Professor, Education
Cape Breton University
Nova Scotia, Canada

KRIS MAGNUSSON

8. NEW TECHNOLOGIES AND LEADERSHIP CHALLENGES FOR TEACHER EDUCATION

If one job of public education is to prepare young people for the future, then the rate of change in today's society makes that task daunting, especially when we insist on following static models of education. Recently, Forbes magazine (Casserly, 2012) published a list of jobs that did not exist 10 years ago; the list included "market research data miner," "social media manager," and "chief listening officer." In the United Kingdom, a panel of futurists created "the 20 most popular jobs in 2030"; the list included gems such as "nano-mechanic," "old-age wellness manager," and "memory augmentation surgeon" (First News, 2014). Preparing young people for an unknown and unpredictable future will require new mindsets, strategies and processes for our teachers.

Educational technology is often heralded as the critical link for educational change, and it is usually thought of in terms of digital devices and systems. A more traditional conception of technology is derived from the Greek root words "techne" meaning an art, skill or craft, and "logia" or the "the study of." Hence, "technology" is simply the study of the ways of doing things. Wikipedia (2014) defines technology as "the usage and knowledge of tools, machines, techniques, crafts, systems and methods of organization, *in order to solve a problem*" [italics added]. Too often, discussions of C21 learning focus on the wrong problem: "How do we better integrate digital technology into K-12 education?" A much better problem statement is, "How do we improve student learning and create personal pathways to the future?" This then begs a related problem: How do we bring new attitudes, ideas and practices into our places of learning?

It is incumbent upon those in educational leadership to avoid falling into C21 rhetoric and to instead remain focused on broader conceptions of effective educational practice and technology. The rapidly changing contexts of the classroom pose a fundamental challenge for teacher education programs: to prepare students to develop and adapt ways to solve problems—that is, to develop and employ technologies—and not to simply replicate existing teaching practices. Educational leaders will increasingly be called upon to create opportunities for members of educational communities to develop sophistication in at least five "core technologies."

First, the heart of teaching excellence lies in the nature of the relationships that are created between teacher and learner. Too often, while acknowledging the centrality of the role of relationship in personal change, we assume that by disposition (e.g., a caring attitude) and general character (e.g., a will to improve the life of others) beginning teachers will somehow naturally form effective bonds with students. However, as we have learned from the field of counsellor education, caring is a necessary but insufficient condition to effect change. The development of highly effective working alliances involves a relational technology—a process that increases the likelihood of engagement in the learning process through relational means.

Second, we need to develop competence in cultural technology. Our most pressing need for technological advancement lies in the need for bridging cultural divides. The "industrial" model of education was designed as an efficient delivery mechanism, not an efficient learning mechanism. What limited successes the system did have depended largely on a mono-cultural audience. Sue and Sue (1999) describe the devastating effects of "ethnocentric monoculturalism" in which individuals demonstrate an unconscious valuing of their cultural perspective over all others. We must continue to explore methods for the respectful inclusion of a variety of cultural histories and experiences within the classroom, and to deeply interrogate our own assumptions and biases. Furthermore, we need to find ways to bridge sub-cultural divides that may be even more problematic than ethnic or geographically determined cultures. In a presentation to educators, Ross Laird (personal communication, May 7, 2010) described the great divide between young people (as represented by "geek" culture) and pre-Web 3.0 people. His definition of geek, as "one who chooses concentration over conformity … and thrives on imagination and knowledge" describes an individual from a technology-immersed sub-culture for whom our traditional ways of educating are almost completely irrelevant. Our teaching strategies must increasingly respect idiosyncratic ways of being, and to do so we will need to develop methods that create awareness of our own assumptions, values and biases, that help us to understand the worldview of the culturally different, and to then design appropriate strategies, techniques and experiences that will effect learning (Sue & Sue, 1999).

The third technology we need to embrace is career technology. Most people still think of "career" in terms of occupational choice. However, it is better conceptualized as the constellation of life-roles a person plays over a lifetime. It is a way of living intentionally in the present so as to help shape a preferred future, and involves four interrelated constructs that we have called "coherent career practice" (Magnusson & Redekopp, 2008). *Career literacy* develops capacity for acquiring and making sense of information so that people can make choices that will benefit them in the future. *Career gumption* instills hope, and builds and sustains the enthusiasm, energy and will to be adaptive in a changing world. *Career context* helps people see how they might fit into this world, and to achieve a balance between personal needs and the forces and influences that surround their daily lives. Finally, *career integrity* helps people find ways to make decisions and take actions in ways that allow them to maintain a sense of identity, connectedness and pride in what they do. Personalized learning cannot succeed without creating personalized pathways for learners, and there is a need for teacher education programs to embed coherent career practice within their core programs.

The fourth technology is "core teaching" technology. John Dewey (1916) emphasized the role of communication as a sharing of experience until the experience is shared between two or more parties. Despite the different context that C21 presents for learning, the notion of "sharing experience" remains as strong today as it did nearly a century ago, and begs the question, "what experiences are worth sharing, and how do we best do that?" Furthermore, if sharing of experience is the basis of learning, then the greatest threat to learning—and hence the greatest need for "teaching technology," is to be cut off from sharing. From my experience in counselling and teaching, students who are at risk experience alienation, which comes in three forms that often intersect: to be cut off from one's past; to be cut off from one's present; and to be cut off from one's future. If one or more of these sources of alienation are working in young people's lives, they become at risk for not succeeding in our educational systems. And this is where truly transformative education comes in: quality education is defined by our success in "sharing experiences," not the range of our techniques or the sophistication of our technology. Good education always has and always will be about four simple constructs: identification of individual learning needs; understanding of the unique contexts in which the learner is situated; identification of learning resources available; and making creative connections between and among these factors to foster growth and development. While learning contexts and resources are in constant flux, the need for strong learning relationships remains constant. Thus, the most effective "technologies" of teaching practice are those that enable relationships, and thus understanding, through sharing of experience.

The final "technology" needed to support educational practice is one that we have struggled mightily with as a profession: the technology of impact assessment. There are two seemingly competing views of educational impact assessment. At the system level, the focus tends to be on "accountability" through broad achievement results (e.g., how well are our grade 4 students doing in math). At the level where services are actually delivered—that is, the teacher in the classroom—the focus tends to be on observable and developmental change, and evaluation "of and for" learning. Both views are important and relevant, but we need to continue to develop our measurement attitudes and technologies to ensure that we are documenting and reporting on the things that really matter in public education. In addition to achievement measures, we need to better document and report on sources of engagement (i.e., hope and confidence, which are antidotes to alienation), learning attitudes (i.e., the will and desire to learn), learning strategies (how to learn is more important than what to learn), and learning gains (i.e., personal growth).

A PREFERRED FUTURE FOR TEACHER EDUCATION

If we are to embrace the need for teaching practice to encompass a suite of "technologies"—of ways of solving educational problems—then the nature of teacher education programs will need to change. Most of our educational programs, divided into a series of courses and practicum experiences, exemplify what I call replicating systems. Our focus is largely on what has worked in the past, and our structures are designed to replicate that success. This is an entirely sensible approach, as long as things don't change too much. However, in times of change, we need to focus on present and future needs, and our core task must be on reinventing success (not reproducing success). It is somewhat ironic that teacher education programs often have radical roots, but then year after year retain the structures and forms that were present at inception. These structures become "iconified" and in the process, the creative process is lost. Of course, this is not a problem specific to teacher education programs; sadly, universities are often the first to discover and the last to adopt new ways.

There are a variety of structures for teacher education programs across Canada, and each has its merits and drawbacks. In most cases, programs were developed to maximize educational impact within the constraints of the university structures that contained them. How education is delivered is more likely to be driven by the mechanisms by which the university issues degrees, tracks credits, organizes semesters, and assigns workloads than it is by the needs for professional learning. One feature of a preferred future for teacher education is that we continue to push back against the tyranny of structures that were designed for other times and purposes, and instead imagine how we might better foster adaptability, creativity and the development of multifaceted technological practice. Integrated practicum experiences, flexible learning environments, the blurring of traditional semester-based timetabling, and focusing on outputs (results of learning) rather than inputs (credit hours, course titles, etc.) will nudge us towards that preferred future. A critical leadership challenge will be to foster the creative within the boundaries of the possible.

Whilst we are busy imagining a preferred future, we must be careful to retain those elements from our past experience that are most likely to continue to work in the future. Admission processes still need to attend to character and dispositions of applicants in addition to academic qualifications. Professional educators still benefit from solid "foundations of teaching practice" such as learning processes, the social and individual contexts of learning, and the design and management of curriculum. Relational and reflective practices still need to take precedence over strategies for content management; we teach people not subjects. The capacity to develop effective working alliances—with children, colleagues, parents, etc.—and the will to continuously examine and improve one's own practice are still more relevant to teaching practice than the acquisition of larger tool kits of discipline-specific strategies and resources. Finally, quality time in supervised practice (with effective feedback) is still essential preparation for entering the teaching profession.

Two additional challenges—and thus opportunities—for teacher education programs are on the near horizon. First, teacher education programs must play a more active, intentional and integrated role in induction processes. Second, we must focus on the continuum of teaching practice, and devise more integrated strategies for pre-service and in-service education. If we truly embrace the "life-long learning" mantra, we must be prepared to work in collaboration with school districts and professional teacher associations to design and deliver opportunities for continued professional development, seamless transitions through phases of teaching practice and the creation of spaces for co-constructing knowledge of and contributions to teaching practice.

There is a rich and wonderful tradition of teacher education programs in Canada, and we can be proud of our contributions to educational practice. However, while we need to retain those core elements that work well, we also need to imagine and integrate new ways of engaging developing teachers. This may mean stepping away from the comfortable structures and assumptions of past practice and adopting the beliefs and practices of truly innovating systems.

REFERENCES

Casserly, M. (2012). *10 jobs that didn't exist 10 years ago*. Retrieved from http://www.forbes.com/sites/meghancasserly/2012/05/11/10-jobs-that-didnt-exist-10-years-ago/

Dewey, J. (1916). *Democracy and education*. New York, NY: MacMillan.

First News. (2014). *The 20 most popular jobs in 2030*. Retrieved from http://www.firstnews.co.uk/news-in-pictures/the-20-most-popular-jobs-in-2030-i48/the-most-popular-jobs-in-2030-p514

Magnusson, K., & Redekopp, D. (2008, April). *The challenge of coherent career practice*. Paper presented at CANNEXUS 2008 (National Career Development Conference), Montreal, QC.

Sue, D. W., & Sue, D. (1999). *Counseling the culturally different*. New York, NY: John Wiley and Sons.

Wikipedia (2014), Retrieved from http://en.wikipedia.org/wiki/Technology

Kris Magnusson
Faculty of Education
Simon Fraser University
British Columbia, Canada

DAVID MANDZUK

9. WALKING THE TIGHTROPE

Staying Upright in Turbulent Times

INTRODUCTION

The purpose of this essay is to share my perspective on trying to lead responsibly as a dean of education and to walk the tightrope that is inherent in the role. By "walking the tightrope," I mean trying to balance the internal pressures from inside the institution with the external pressures that are increasingly having an impact on how that role is played out. In fact, I would compare my limited time as a dean to an academic high-wire act where sudden, unexpected distractions have threatened to knock me off balance. One thing I have learned is that in order to stay upright during these turbulent times in faculties of education, I will need to be keenly aware of challenges and trends that are having an increasing impact on how deans of education perceive their roles now and in the future.

In the first part of the essay, I discuss what I think are three of the most common challenges facing Canadian deans of education. They are: a) managing the uneasy partnership between our various stakeholders and our faculties, b) being a member of the university's senior executive team while still advocating for our faculties, and c) listening to faculty delegates while encouraging them to think and act like university trustees.

In the second part of the essay, I focus on three trends that I have observed as a dean of education. These are: a) the stronger emphasis on external relations, rather than just attending to internal matters, b) the increasing need to generate new sources of revenue rather than attending mainly to academic matters, and c) the obligation to think about succession planning for the future, not just working in the present.

In the final part of the essay, I will consider these points together and suggest what deans of education need to be mindful of in their efforts to walk the tightrope of their work, stay upright in the process, and create a vision for their faculties of education.

COMMON CHALLENGES

One of the common challenges facing deans of education is the increasing need for them to be involved with external stakeholders like superintendents, trustees, provincial teachers' associations, and government in the formal and informal regulation and delivery of teacher education (Crocker & Dibbon, 2008; Young,

Hall, & Clarke, 2007). Although from one perspective it is encouraging that so many people feel vested in improving teacher education, from another perspective it can be disillusioning when the list of people you need to consult with seems to go on forever. Tom (1997) sums up this dilemma best when he states that "in many ways, everyone is in charge of teacher education, yet nobody is" (p. 7). Not only can the involvement of stakeholder groups be seen as overstepping and threatening the autonomy of faculties of education, our stakeholders do not typically offer any additional resources when they try to influence program requirements. While this can create resentment among our colleagues, in my opinion, deans have an obligation to work collaboratively with all those who feel they should have a voice in how teachers are prepared. I also think that deans need to help their faculty colleagues realize that sometimes, our external stakeholders and government get involved because they have little faith that if left to our own devices, we will make the changes that are needed to our programs. A good example of this was our Ministry's mandate that faculties of education in the province require all B. Ed. students to complete a compulsory course in Aboriginal education in order to be certified to teach. Theoretically, most faculty members would agree that our students need to have a greater awareness of the history of Aboriginal people in Canada; however, at a more practical level, they don't necessarily appreciate having others "interfere" with the content of academic programs and they certainly don't want to have to give up the courses they teach in order to make room for such a requirement.

Another common challenge that deans experience stems from having to function as a member of the university's senior executive team while simultaneously, advocating for their respective faculties (see Gmelch, Wolverton, Wolverton, & Sarros, 1999). This balancing act is not an easy one as the two agendas do not easily coexist. For example, as a dean, I have been expected to support the implementation of new university-wide systems changes such as a new computerized travel and expense claim program, a centralized room booking program, and shared printing services that have discouraged the use of personal printers in faculty offices. Predictably, as those systems have been launched, I have heard from faculty and staff about how these changes have resulted in more, not less, work and increased workplace stress. Even though most of us know about the "implementation dip" (Fullan, 2001) characterized by the inevitable tensions that people experience as they learn new processes and procedures for the first time, faculty and staff still expect the dean to take their concerns seriously. They also expect the dean to make the case to the senior executive team that people need more support in managing the change process and/or slowing down the pace of the change altogether.

A third challenge that deans confront on almost a daily basis exists between what Dickeson (2010) and Fox and Shotts (2007) refer to as *delegates*, those faculty members who advocate only for their own specific interests as opposed to *trustees*, those faculty members who, in spite of their own specific interests, are more able and more willing to consider the needs of the faculty and the entire university. Although everyone's interests are important, some are more strategically important than others because they are priorities for the faculty and the university. Deans must be able to persuade delegates that in order to be able to access limited resources, we must align our priorities with those of our universities; otherwise, we risk being further marginalized on our campuses. For example, our university recently went through a year-long exercise of identifying "signature research areas," the broad areas of research in which the university already has existing strength and the areas on which it wants to stake its reputation. Some faculty members were incensed with what they saw as a top-down attempt to restrict what they wanted to study and research. They urged me to resist such attempts and to strike out on our own but my counter-argument was that going out on our own would come at the cost of being taken less seriously by the rest of the university.

DEVELOPING TRENDS

Along with the common challenges discussed above, it is important to keep in mind that deans of education are serving at a time when new trends are starting to surface. One developing trend is the increasing emphasis being placed on external relations with government and the media. As Hunt (2012) suggests, there was a day when deans spent most of their time engaged in internal relations working with faculty and students on primarily academic matters; however, with decreasing government and university funding and increased scrutiny of educational issues in the popular media, deans have had to become external ambassadors for, not just internal managers of, their faculties. Although external activities can be gratifying and ultimately beneficial, it is very easy for deans to feel conflicted about the amount of time they need to spend outside rather than inside their faculties. For example, recently, I had to miss a student orientation that I would normally have attended because I had to meet with the Deputy Minister who wanted to know how the deans of education in the province were planning to respond to the public criticism over Math education. Although I would have preferred to meet with our students on that day, I also knew that I needed to represent the faculty on this increasingly contentious issue in our province.

Another developing trend has been the increased emphasis on fundraising or what is commonly called *development work* (Hunt, 2012). This kind of work is important because at a time of reduced budgets, monies raised externally might be the only way that faculties can hope to launch new initiatives. Unfortunately, very few deans of education are experts in this kind of fundraising. According to Hunt (2012, p. 4) "some academics love development work and are highly effective at it. It comes naturally to them and they happily make it a high priority. Others tolerate it, engaging somewhat hesitatingly and reluctantly. Still others avoid it at all costs. Not surprisingly, those in the first category are the most successful and raise the most money." It is easy to think of this kind of work as superfluous but, as I have come to realize, if deans are expected to move their faculties forward by developing new programs, renovating physical spaces, and improving the quality of life for students, they must engage in development work if those kinds of initiatives have a hope of getting off the ground.

A final developing trend that deans must increasingly attend to is capacity building and succession planning in their faculties. I find that fewer and fewer of our colleagues seem to want to step up to play leadership roles in our faculties and I think there are a number of reasons for this trend. Experienced faculty members are often reluctant because they know that it will mean having to deal with issues that they'd rather not deal with, having less autonomy over how they come and go, and quite frankly, having to serve the institution's needs more than their own. Newer faculty members, on the other hand, are reluctant because they tend to be preoccupied with getting their teaching and research agendas up and running (a message they hear loud and clear from others). They are also worried that if they do step into leadership roles earlier than expected, their work in these roles won't actually "count" when they apply for tenure and promotion. It seems to me that deans need to address these kinds of issues directly and to assure new faculty that if they do serve the faculty in these kinds of roles, their work will be valued and acknowledged down the road.

It makes one wonder if this trend in developing leadership capacity within our own faculties is related to the increasing challenge in finding deans on the national stage. Increasingly, one hears how the pool of potential deans is becoming smaller (see Gmelch, Wolverton, Wolverton, & Sarros, 1999) and that it is becoming more difficult to find people who are able and willing to take on these demanding roles. If there is a connection between these two trends, then one wonders who will be willing to walk the tightrope in the future.

CREATING A VISION

Keeping these challenges and trends in mind, I think that as deans of education trying to create visions for the future of our faculties, it is clear that we need to be thinking outwards rather than inwards. Furthermore, we need to be taking the long view rather than just being preoccupied with the here and now. In other words, if we are to have a chance of walking the tightrope inherent in the dean's role and actually making it to the other side still standing, we need to be working alongside government, external stakeholders, alumni, donors and other units on campus. We will also need to be identifying, nurturing, and supporting our potential leaders and giving them opportunities to take on leadership roles for short periods of time on a temporary basis. While the waters may often be turbulent below us, the only way that we, as deans, can create a vision for our faculties is by continuing to focus on the way ahead, encouraging those around us to think beyond their own self-interests, and working toward a common goal that will position us more strategically to face the challenges of the future.

REFERENCES

Crocker, R., & Dibbon, D. (2008). *Teacher education in Canada.* Kelowna, BC: Society for the Advancement of Excellence in Education.

Dickeson, R. C. (2010). *Prioritizing academic programs and services: Reallocating resources to achieve strategic balance.* San Francisco, CA: Jossey-Bass.

Fox, J., & Shotts, K. W. (2007). Delegates or trustees? A theory of political accountability. *The Journal of Politics, 71,* 1225-1237.

Fullan, M. (2001). *Leading in a culture of change.* San Francisco, CA: Jossey-Bass.

Gmelch, W. H., Wolverton, M., Wolverton, M. L., & Sarros, J. C. (1999). The academic dean: An imperilled species searching for balance. *Research in Higher Education, 40,* 717-740.

Hunt, P. C. (2012). *Development for academic leaders: A practical guide for fundraising success.* San Francisco, CA: Jossey-Bass.

Tom, A. (1997). *Redesigning teacher education.* New York, NY: New York Press.

Young, J., Hall, C., & Clarke, T. (2007). Challenges to university autonomy in initial teacher education programmes: The cases of England, Manitoba, and British Columbia. *Teaching & Teacher Education, 23,* 81-93.

David Mandzuk
Faculty of Education
University of Manitoba
Manitoba, Canada

KEN W. MCCLUSKEY

10. REFLECTING AND ACTING ON REFLECTION AND ACTION[1]

Mobilizing Teacher Education for Social Justice

It has been well over a decade since some of us seasoned veterans in education at the University of Winnipeg (UW) had our first conversation concerning the need to reach out to the community around us. The facts were inescapable: We are the inner-city university—the campus that sits in the heart of downtown, surrounded by all the "typical" core-area problems. Entering our institution each day, the faculty and staff see firsthand the desperation of homelessness, the degradation of drugs, and the desolation of life in youth gangs. These realities confront us as we arrive each morning, and as we return with caution (some using "safe walk") to our vehicles in the evening.

A FACULTY IDENTITY

For those involved in that initial discussion, it seemed obligatory to strive to become more a part of, not apart from, the challenges of our immediate environs. Yes, we had a responsibility to do the things a good education program does: To deliver solid curriculum, instruction, and assessment courses; to add an abundance of other relevant offerings into the hopper; and to build upon theoretical foundations by putting in place strong practicum experiences for our teachers-to-be. But we wanted to be more than merely a "good" program. In a quest for improvement and social relevance, then, our mandate gradually grew to encompass urban, inner-city issues; our mission broadened to include contributing to the community; and our identity coalesced around the themes of justice, equality, and enrichment and talent development for all, including populations that had been hitherto marginalized. In the process of forging this expanded identity, new courses were developed that emphasized "all of the above," outreach projects were launched (starting with some significant mentoring ventures), and practicum was reconfigured to take advantage of and feature the unique opportunities that abound in inner-city classrooms. Over time, we found it surprisingly natural to build upon

---

[1] Reprinted in revised form with permission from ICIE. The original chapter by Ken W. McCluskey (2013), entitled Reflecting and Acting on Reflection and Action, appeared in L. Sokal & K. W. McCluskey (Eds.), *Community Connections: Reaching Out From the Ivory Tower* (pp. 241-248). Ulm, Germany: International Centre for Innovation in Education.

local initiatives and, in an effort to instill a spirit of true global citizenship within our students, to move on to service delivery projects on an international scale.

Several of our faculty and colleagues have been guided in their efforts by Bronfenbrenner (1979), whose insight has provided much of the theoretical rationale for reaching out. Substantive ideas to build upon also came from the service learning literature itself and, relatedly, from Robert Greenleaf's (1998, 2002) conception of servant leadership. As well, members of our faculty have spent a lot of time together thinking about creativity, purpose, and altruism in leadership, and how to serve in meaningful fashion (McCluskey, 2013).

EMPATHY AND SUPPORT FOR THE UNDERDOG

In any case, as a faculty, we decided to accept the moral obligation and stretch our jurisdiction by providing stronger preparation for our pre-service teachers in the area of at-risk, inner-city education, and—as part of the process—to contribute directly by offering more outreach services aimed at vulnerable children and youth. We injected a liberal dose of "social capital" theory into the program (Bergsgaard, 2013: Putnam, 2000), along with specific training in approaches such as Creative Problem Solving (CPS) (Treffinger, Isaksen, & Stead-Dorval, 2006), Life Space Crisis Intervention (LSCI) (Long, Wood, & Fecser, 2001), Response Ability Pathways (RAP) (Brendtro & du Toit, 2005), the Circle of Courage (Brendtro, Brokenleg, & Van Bockern, 1990), and the like. Courses and practical real-world opportunities in mentoring and service learning followed.

Aside from the specific "how-to" training involved, we identified a number of guiding principles for those working with at-risk young people:

- Be nice. With all the techniques, approaches, and programs available, it is astounding how often educators neglect this basic method for reaching out to relationship-resistant youngsters. Nicholas Long (1997), a pioneer in the area of at-risk children and youth, has written about the "therapeutic power of kindness." Echoing his sentiments, Aldous Huxley apparently once remarked, "It is a little embarrassing that, after 45 years of research and study, the best advice I can give to people is to be a little kinder to each other." The notion espoused by some hard-line instructors that "Students don't have to like you!" isn't universally (or even usually) true. Relationship building matters a great deal, especially when working with troubled, troubling students (Brendtro, Brokenleg, & Van Bockern, 1990; Pestalozzi, 1951). Indeed, in many ways, "Relationships ... are the intervention" (Gharabaghi, 2008, p. 31).
- Take time. In our fast-paced world, everybody seems to be scurrying hither and yon at a frenetic pace. We're ruled by time, even though it's artificial—a mere construct (Charleston, 1989). Somehow, we allow ourselves to be governed by something we've created: We buy, borrow, steal, and make time; we have downtime, uptime, and overtime; and we rationalize not spending enough of each day with our children and grandchildren by saying that later we will make it up to them by providing "quality time." According to Fromm (1956),

relationship is not a feeling; it's an action. For Brendtro, Brokenleg, and Van Bockern (1990) it's an "endurance event." The point is simply that, if we want to play a meaningful role in somebody's life, we have take the time to be there—to get down in the trenches and make real connections (McCluskey & McCluskey, 2000).

- Strive to understand. All too often we are unwilling to take what de Bono (1973) and others have referred to as the "other point of view" (OPV). When confronted with contentious issues, too few people make a legitimate attempt to understand the other voice. Simply presenting a few "opposing" words will serve to illustrate the insurmountable gulf that often lies between antagonistic perspectives: Witness Atheist-Catholic, Pro-Life-Pro-Choice, Israeli-Palestinian, English Canadian-French Canadian, etc., etc., *ad infinitum*. While one should not blindly accept somebody else's viewpoint, the basis for true problem solving is, in fact, to take the place of the other. In education, for example, it is important to realize that the reality and worldview of at-risk children is not necessarily the same as that of the majority of their teachers: How relevant are our middle-class standards, codes of conduct, and curricula for a 10-year-old who has witnessed alcoholism and violence in the home, experienced physical and sexual abuse, and been bumped from pillar to post in the school system?
- Let them help. It is not uncommon for teachers working with needy students to provide an overabundance of helping. With the best will in the world, they offer extra tutoring, resource time, problem solving training, anger management sessions, and so on. However, if one is always the helpee and never the helper, it can become subtly dehumanizing (McCluskey, 2000). Curwin (2007) has observed that one of the best ways to engage vulnerable students is by letting them practice genuine altruism. Allowing them to help others develops responsibility, empathy, and satisfaction. And certainly, there is an abundance of literature that points to the value of empowering at-risk children and youth through service learning activities (Brendtro & du Toit, 2005; Brendtro, Mitchell, & McCall, 2009; Brendtro & Shahbazian, 2004; Kapp, 2009). As well, concrete project possibilities abound in programs such as the Community Problem Solving component of the Future Problem Solving Program (FPSP).
- Recast reality. It's sometimes too easy to emphasize the downside when dealing with difficult young people: Concerned with day-to-day survival, parents and educators may have a tendency to address only the negative and miss all the good stuff. By refocusing and looking at things in a different way, we can often identify and nurture the strengths of problem students (McCluskey & McCluskey, 2001). And it's so much easier to move on to the weaknesses if the strengths are highlighted first. Teachers should always be "talent spotters," looking for the unique gifts of all students, even the challenging ones (Young, 1995).

KEN W. MCCLUSKEY

WHAT CAN AND SHOULD UNIVERSITIES DO?

Lest we be accused of hubris, it is necessary to state that our faculty members are not so presumptuous as to try to change the world; we simply want to do our part with respect to inner-city education, sustainability, Aboriginal issues, community outreach, and global citizenship and responsibility. Incidentally, although professors from all disciplines at our institution value and participate in some very significant community projects, we are not advocating that all faculty engage in community outreach activities. There is plenty of room for different perspectives and roles at university: Not everyone should do the same things in the same ways. Many serve best by devoting their time, energy, and talent to teaching or doing research on campus.

Be that as it may, we believe the faculty of education ought to take the lead when it comes to community service. By virtue of who we are and what we do, it makes sense for our people to devote considerable time to collaborating directly with schools, agencies, and neighbourhood groups. As noted elsewhere, we would do well to consider education as taking place within an "ecosystem of learning," in which many components contribute to the goals of success and productivity and interact in interdependent ways. In addition to schools and classrooms, education is influenced by what happens in homes; at computers on the Internet; in community workplaces; in churches, museums, and theaters; on athletic fields; and in correctional facilities, youth homes, and health-care centers (McCluskey & Treffinger, 1998, p. 218).

It should also be mentioned that community service is an extremely risky business. In leaving the safety of the tower, faculty expose themselves to the vagaries of external-to-the-university problems, the politics of the field, and criticism from other sources. And no matter how carefully real-life interventions may be designed on the drawing board, we've found that things usually don't work out as planned—one typically winds up flying by the seat of one's pants. Occasionally too, we've been criticized for exaggerating and making programs out to be something more than what they are. We're okay with that, for we've learned that sometimes you have to erect a facade to get things started. With time, stick-to-itiveness, and a continued infusion of support, however, it is possible eventually to fill in that facade and create something very special.

Currently, our education faculty is in the midst of an internal program review, which we see not as a one-off event, but rather as a never-ending, work-in-progress process of reflection and action. In charting the way forward, we understand that our program must look ahead, become even more global, and continue to evolve in flexible ways. In support of that evolution, we now seek to develop broader international networks, disseminate information more widely, and provide tangible training opportunities for students, faculty, and educators in the schools.

To this end, the University of Winnipeg recently entered into partnership with the International Centre for Innovation in Education (ICIE) in Ulm, Germany. With the help of ICIE, we are preparing a proposal for a formal M.Ed. program of our own in the area of at-risk education and have just established a *Lost Prizes* International (LPI) Centre on campus to help teachers engage unengaged students.

Increasingly, more and more of our faculty will have an opportunity to play major roles in conferences worldwide, and share their work in the new UW/LPI/ICIE *International Journal for Talent Development and Creativity* and through monographs and books published by ICIE. Last year, as part of the collaboration, we introduced the *Lost Prizes*/ICIE Seminars, which henceforth will welcome a number of international scholars and participants to UW each July. A corollary feature of the Seminars is the unique conference-connected Post-Baccalaureate Diploma in Education courses.

It's recognized that we haven't yet attained Nirvana—there are certainly imperfections in much of what we do. Still, the alternative—to attempt nothing—is unpalatable. Looking at all the service and community outreach initiatives at the University of Winnipeg (Lamoureux, McCluskey, Wiebe, & Baker, 2008; Sokal & McCluskey, 2013; Sutherland & Sokal, 2003), we, as a faculty collectively, are decidedly proud of what we have wrought to date and of what we envision for the future.

REFERENCES

Bergsgaard, M. (2013). *A Zen companion in a just and effective classroom*. Ulm, Germany: International Centre for Innovation in Education.

Brendtro, L. K., & du Toit, L. (2005). *Response ability pathways: Restoring bonds of respect*. Capetown, South Africa: Pretext Publishers.

Brendtro, L. K., & Shahbazian, M. (2004). *Troubled children and youth: Turning problems into opportunities*. Champaign, IL, Research Press.

Brendtro, L. K., Brokenleg, M., & Van Bockern, S. (1990). *Reclaiming youth at risk: Our hope for the future*. Bloomington, IN: National Educational Service.

Brendtro, L. K., Mitchell, M. L., & McCall, H. J. (2009). *Deep brain learning: Pathways to potential with challenging youth*. Albion, MI: Starr Commonwealth.

Bronfenbrenner, U. (1979). *The ecology of human development: Experiments by nature and design*. Cambridge, MA: Harvard University Press.

Charleston, S. (1989). The tyranny of time. *Lutheran Woman Today, 2*(7), 27-32.

Curwin, R. L. (2007). *Rediscovering hope: Our greatest teaching strategy*. Bloomington, IN: Solution Tree.

de Bono, E. (1973). *CoRT thinking*. Blandford Forum, Dorset, U.K.: Direct Education Services.

Fromm, E. (1956). *The art of loving*. New York, NY: Harper and Row.

Gharabaghi, K. (2008). Reclaiming our 'toughest' youth. *Reclaiming Children and Youth, 17*(3), 30-32.

Greenleaf, R. K. (1998). *The power of servant leadership*. San Francisco, CA: Berrett-Koehler.

Greenleaf, R. K. (2002). *Servant leadership: A journey into the nature of legitimate power and greatness*. Mahwah, NJ: Paulist Press.

Kapp, A. (2009). Empowering young people through service. YouthBuild Philadelphia, a YouthBuild AmeriCorps program. *Reclaiming Children and Youth, 18*(1), 8-11.

Lamoureux, K., McCluskey, K. W., Wiebe, A., & Baker, P. A. (Eds.). (2008). *Mentoring in a Canadian context*. Winnipeg, Manitoba: Institute of Urban Studies, The University of Winnipeg.

Long, N. J. (1997). The therapeutic power of kindness. *Reclaiming Children and Youth, 5* (4), 242-246.

Long, N. J., Wood, M. M., & Fecser, F. A. (2001). *Life space intervention: Talking with students in conflict* (2nd ed.). Austin, TX: PRO-ED.

McCluskey, K. W. (2000). Lines in the sand: Are students with difficulties being forced from our schools? *Reaching Today's Youth, 4*(4), 28-33.

McCluskey, K. W. (2013). *Thoughts about tone, educational leadership, and building creative climates in our schools* (2nd ed.). Ulm, Germany: International Centre for Innovation in Education.

McCluskey, K. W., & McCluskey, A. L. A. (2000). Gray matters: The power of grandparent involvement. *Reclaiming Children and Youth, 9*(2), 111-115.

McCluskey, K. W., & McCluskey, A. L. A. (2001). *Understanding ADHD: Our personal journey.* Winnipeg, MB: Portage & Main Press.

McCluskey, K. W., & Treffinger, D. J. (1998). Nurturing talented but troubled children and youth. *Reclaiming Children and Youth, 6*(4), 215-219, 226.

Pestalozzi, J. (1951). *The education of man: Aphorisms.* New York, NY: Philosophical Library.

Putnam, R. (2000). *Bowling alone: The collapse and revival of American community.* New York, NY: Simon and Schuster.

Sokal, L., & McCluskey, K. W. (Eds.). (2013). *Community connections: Reaching out from the ivory tower.* Ulm, Germany: International Centre for Innovation in Education.

Sutherland, D. L., & Sokal, L. (Eds.). (2003). *Resiliency and capacity building in inner-city learning communities* (pp. 117-126). Winnipeg, MB: Portage & Main Press.

Treffinger, D. J., Isaksen, S. G., & Stead-Dorval, K. B. (2006). *Creative problem solving: An introduction* (4th ed.). Waco, TX: Prufrock Press.

Young, G. C. (1995). Becoming a talent spotter. *Creative Learning Today, 5*(1), 4-5.

Ken McCluskey
Faculty of Education
The University of Winnipeg
Manitoba, Canada

JAMES MCNINCH

11. WORKING AGAINST THE GRAIN

Leadership for 21st Century Teacher Education

As Dean of the Faculty of Education at the University of Regina, participating in this forum provides an opportunity to reflect on program changes initiated in our faculty and on the political and social context in which these changes are occurring. My point of view is based on Hanna Arendt's proposition (1998) that changes occur in a "contested space" in which tensions are inherent and consensus and direction are always problematic.

In Canada, and in Saskatchewan specifically, educators are today working in a context that ties educational "success" instrumentally to economic engines and is generally dismissive and suspicious of pre-K-12 education and post-secondary education for their own sake. There is little appetite these days for child or student-centred learning based on the premise that each young person has the right to a safe and nurturing environment so that they may grow to be loving, thoughtful, and respectful human beings and engaged citizens. Instead, neo-liberal rhetoric today ties literacy to jobs, productivity, and measurable outcomes. The ranking of provinces on international PISA scores has become a macho "pissing match" among provincial Ministers of Education. Authentic assessment is marginalized in favour of "standards" (Robinson, 2012; Sahlsberg & Hargreaves, 2011).

In this context, what is the leadership role of a dean of education? I will articulate how we continue to work "against the grain" to challenge the assumption that our job is merely to "train" teachers to "deliver" curriculum. Two initiatives are described. One is within the faculty: program changes away from positivist, clinical, and technical teacher-training models tempered by a humanist and relational approach, including initiatives to Indigenize our curriculum and ways of knowing, and to hire new members of faculty who reflect Canada's diversity, as well as supporting and advocating for minorities at the individual and community level within an articulated social justice framework.

The second leadership activity is advocating for the professional identity and autonomy of classroom teachers and school-based administrators. This means working against the grain to educate government, the media, and the public about the complexities, fluidity, and ambiguities of schooling, and of what constitutes learning and teaching. This is a huge and unwieldy mandate for any faculty of education. Working against the grain, however, is important and necessary leadership work in the contested field of public education.

PROGRAM RENEWAL AND SOCIAL JUSTICE

In 2005, our faculty, after a decade-long discussion, finally set up a standing committee responsible for making major changes to pre-service teacher education. In 2013, the first students who were part of the new program graduated with a B.Ed.

The content and pedagogy embedded in former programs reflected a technical and rational approach to teacher education formulated in the fifties and adopted across North America in the 1960s (Capello, 2012). This program reflected an assumption that teacher formation happens best through a process of skill-building and practice. Emphasized were micro-teaching in a "laboratory" setting with peers, with attention paid to subsets of skills such as "wait time" and "equitable distribution of questions," classroom "management," and lessons that were planned in great detail with a formulaic "set, development, and closure" (Lang & Evans, 2006). Particularly at the secondary level, teacher candidates were seen as subject area specialists with content knowledge to impart as teachers of subjects, not teachers of students.

Program Renewal provided us an opportunity to acknowledge many changes in society, including the rise of instructional technology and social media, and changing views of what constitutes knowledge. There was a strong desire to frame teaching as "relational"; pedagogy would emphasize building relations with individual children, engaging them to be motivated to learn about themselves and others and the world in which they live.

Our programs had become silos with no overlap or connection. Students in the elementary program never took classes with students in the secondary program. In the old program a course in educational administration was required of students only in the secondary program. This reflected a 50-year-old assumption that students in the elementary program, predominately female, were not likely candidates for administrative positions and so didn't "need" such a class. Now all our students are introduced to concepts of educational leadership in various contexts.

A similar discrepancy existed where only students in the elementary program required a course in "special education," as if teachers in high schools would not meet students of varied physical and intellectual abilities and therefore would need no preparation to address the adaptive dimension of instruction and to learn how to collaborate as part of interprofessional teams.

Another gap across all programs was that there was no required course on assessment. It was assumed that various methods courses would "cover" this topic, but it was clear that a patch work approach did not give pre-service teachers knowledge of authentic assessment or of distinctions between formative and summative evaluation, or of the strengths and limitations of various normative and criteria-based evaluation models, much less to ask critical questions about the purposes of assessment and evaluation in the first place.

Another feature of the new program is a course that asks the questions "what is curriculum?" and "how and why does it come to be official and enshrined"? One objective is to ensure students understand that much teaching and learning happens beyond the walls of a school. To re-enforce this, our students are required to engage in volunteer service learning in community, rather than in a classroom setting. This allows our students to see children and youth as members of society and not just as "pupils," and helps to contextualize schooling as part of a much broader social construct.

These are only some of the changes implemented, following broad consultation with our education partners in the province. Stakeholders and faculty members alike identified the readiness to engage Aboriginal children and the importance of Aboriginal perspectives as critically important. The new program requires students to take at least one Indigenous studies course, and all students are oriented to Treaty Education mandated K-12 by the provincial government.

Surveys confirmed what we already knew: many graduates are teaching outside of their majors and minors. We address this in a core class that de-emphasizes the role of teacher as expert and focuses on inquiry-based learning where a teacher acts as a facilitator regardless of the age of the students or the subject. This is framed around "place-based" learning which acknowledges the context in which teaching and learning occurs.

We have modified our internship seminar from an expert/novice apprenticeship model to something more akin to guided professional development for both the student intern and the co-operating teacher. This emphasizes that ongoing learning is foundational to the success of every teacher, regardless of years spent in the classroom. This has proven to be a welcome change, particularly for dedicated professionals who volunteer to have student-interns in their classrooms for 4 months every fall.

Faculty attitudes to program renewal varied. Some, motivated by various degrees of inertia, nostalgia, amnesia, and fantasia (Schulman, 2004)), couldn't see the need for such dramatic change. Others seemed prepared to discuss process in perpetuity. A dedicated core of faculty, however, with leadership from associate deans and the dean, made a commitment to renewal and change.

Another aspect of program renewal was a review of our ways of knowing in light of the reticence of our faculty on such issues as white privilege and racism. A recent incident at the University of Regina helped "prove" the persistent need for such re-orientation. The cheerleading team were "caught" in a Twitter photo dressed in mock "cowboy and Indian" costumes complete with the faux paraphernalia of Wild West mythology. There are many ways to critique this performance of racialized whiteness, but it illustrates the ongoing need to help pre-service teachers explore the relationship between the construction of "good teacher" and the larger context in which a teacher becomes a professional (Schick & McNinch, 2009).

The faculty of education has taken a lead in our university in providing direct and indirect ways not only to make this campus more welcoming to First Nations and Métis and Inuit students, but to also ask hard questions about what it might mean to Indigenize the curriculum. Beyond "content," we ask students to ask "what is knowledge, how is it privileged, and who does it benefit and why?" This again, is difficult work that goes against the grain, but the faculty of education has provided leadership in this realm to the entire campus. The Canadian Deans' of Education *Accord on Indigenous Education* (2012) has proved useful in moving this agenda forward.

Program Renewal has allowed a social justice philosophy to explicitly infuse our programs. It has provided us with opportunities to put theory into practice and to support, for example, sexual and gender diversity through the work of Camp fYrefly, a four-day residential experience for queer Saskatchewan youth. This works against the grain of normative discourses that have marginalized gender and sexual diverse students in our schools. We help to build resiliency and leadership skills and to normalize "the other." In turn this has allowed us to position the faculty as a leader, encouraging the Ministry of Education and School Boards in the province to become more inclusive. Recent work with trans-identified and two-spirit youth has been particularly rewarding. Leadership against the grain sometimes means changing the grain itself.

The faculty of education has also collaborated to provide the first Campus for All initiative which welcomes young adults with intellectual disabilities to campus to take one course a semester. After six such semesters these students "graduate" with many new skills, knowledge, and attitudes and are much readier to contribute to the social fabric in meaningful ways. Similarly, our faculty provides a home for Astonished!, a group of young adults with complex physical disabilities who partner with mentors and research the barriers they face every day in mobility and communications. They are trailblazers pushing boundaries by using new technologies and challenging the university to broaden its vision of itself. Such leadership in diversity enriches and enhances us all against the grain.

ADVOCACY FOR TEACHER PROFESSIONALISM: A RESEARCH AGENDA

Faculties of education are not just in the business of providing pre-service and in-service "training" and professional development. Increasingly it has become important to remind our educational partners and the public, that teacher work is not just "labour," and Faculties have a larger role than merely inculcating a series of skills and competencies. It is also about challenging the assumptions about what constitutes the daily professional lives of teachers and advocating for them (Apple, 1989).

A recent study completed by the Regina Faculty of Education (Saskatchewan Teachers' Federation, 2013) provided clear evidence of a growing dissatisfaction of teachers with increased stress, increased accountability, demanding workloads, and a diminution of their roles as professionals. While teachers' commitment to public education and the public good is deeply held, the ethical principles and professional ideals that characterize the roles they wish to perform as teachers is increasingly at risk in the current social, political, and economic climate.

Three themes emerged from this research: a strong sense of teachers' commitment to education, increasingly bigger barriers to teacher and student success, and compromises to teachers' commitment to education. Work intensification refers to teachers being subjected to increasing external pressures, such as demands from policy-makers and broader societal expectations (Larson, 1980). In turn, this results in an increase in the number of tasks or duties for which a teacher is responsible without additional resources or time. As the work of teachers is reduced to executing the decisions made by others, intensification carries a threat of de-professionalism. It becomes, in such a climate, the responsibility of faculties of education to advocate, against the grain, for the importance of teacher autonomy and to encourage the kind of collegial collaboration that will sustain the profession.

Common sense notions that teachers have it "so easy" because of the apparently short school day and school year need unpacking. The public and government officials need to know what we teach to our pre-service teachers: a lack of time for reflection before, during and after teaching is particularly important in an age driven by technologies which have accelerated access to instant information, but have not helped teachers to develop and sustain their relational and pedagogical work with students (Schön, 1983).

Teachers make hundreds of decisions every day about instructional strategies, individual needs of each student, what is important content, how to plan for and assess learning, and how to communicate all this with students, colleagues, administrators and parents. The classroom is a space in which many things are occurring simultaneously, multi-dimensionally, and often unpredictably. Such an environment requires quick thinking in action, but as importantly it requires thoughtful reflection and further planning, adjusting and adapting (Kauchak & Eggen, 2012). This is the invisible work of teachers that we need to explicate, against the grain, to a larger audience. Many educators believe that educational reform will never be successful "if we continue to demean and dishearten the human resource called the teacher on whom so much depends … if we fail to cherish—and challenge—the human heart that is the source of good teaching" (Palmer, 2007).

As educational leaders we need to study the often contradictory public perceptions of the teaching profession. Faculties of education also need to frame the relationship of public education to the development of engaged citizenry and civic, national, and global leadership and of the teaching profession's contribution to the abstract but crucial concept of the "social contract" (Orlowski, 2011).

One only has to think of the politics of high stakes standardized testing as one such contested field where we need to work against the grain, providing evidence-based "proof" of the dangers inherent in focusing on testing and not on learning. Another example is the often ill-informed debate, currently receiving much press (Anderssen, 2014) about the "math wars" and the supposedly lamentable skill level of children who do not know their times-tables. Such arguments quickly default to a false binary between rote learning versus discovery learning. Educators must lead this debate, providing constructive research and dialogue related to the history of math education, issues of gender and technology, and the issue of math as a symbolic language that functions on multiple levels.

CONCLUSION

The neo-liberal agenda of many governments operating in Canada today has presumed that politicians are not just our elected representatives, but rather are to be "managers" of society, reflected in a lean ideology of greater efficiency and productivity. As citizens, as professionals in educational institutions, and as students in schools, we are regarded by government as something to manage, as if we were items on the assembly line that can be fixed and improved (C. Schick, personal communication, March 28, 2014). As academic activists in education, our job is to contribute to the debate and critique of and research into public policy and school practice, for the sake of children in schools (Spooner, in press). Aligning our programs to the diversity of our school populations must go hand-in-hand with our support and advocacy for the professionalism of the teachers we educate who take up positions in schools and who also find themselves for many reasons, working against the grain.

REFERENCES

Anderssen, E. (2014, March 1). Why the war over math is distracting and futile. *The Globe and Mail*. Retrieved from http://www.theglobeandmail.com/news/national/education/why-the-war-over-math-is-distracting-and-futile/article17178295/

Apple, M. (1989). *Teachers and texts: A political economy of class and gender relations in education*. New York, NY: Routledge.

Arendt, H. (1998). *The human condition* (2nd ed.). Chicago, IL: University of Chicago Press.

Cappello, M. (2012). *Producing (white) teachers: A genealogy of secondary teacher education in Regina*. Unpublished dissertation. Regina, SK: University of Regina.

Kauchak, D., & P. Eggen. (2012). *Learning and teaching: Research based methods*. New York, NY: Pearson.

Lang, H., & Evans, D. (2006). *Models, strategies, and methods for effective teaching*. Toronto, ON: Pearson.

Larson, M. (1980). Proletarianization and educated labour. *Theory and Society*, 9, 1.

Palmer, P. (2007). *The courage to teach: Exploring the inner landscape of a teacher's life*. New York, NY: Jossey-Bass.

Orlowski, P. (2011). *Teaching about hegemony: Race, class & democracy in the 21st century*. New York, NY: Springer.

Robinson, K. (2012). *Do schools kill creativity?* TED Talks [Electronic resource] New York, NY: Films Media Group.

Salsberg, P., & Hargreaves, A. (2011). *Finish lessons: What can the world learn from educational change in Finland*. New York, NY: Teachers' College Press.

Saskatchewan Teachers' Federation. (2013). *Teacher time: a study of the challenges of intensification of Saskatchewan Teachers' professional time*. Saskatoon: STF.

Schick, C., & McNinch, J. (2009). Introduction. In C. Schick & J. McNinch (Eds.), *"I thought Pocahontas was a movie": perspectives on race/culture binaries in education and service professions* (pp. iii-v). Regina, SK: CPRC.

Schön, D. (1983). *The reflective practitioner: How professionals think in action*. New York, NY: Basic Books.

Shulman, L. (2004). *Teaching as community property: Essays on higher education*. San Francisco, CA: Jossey-Bass.

Spooner, M. (in press). The deleterious personal and societal effects of the audit culture and a domesticated academy. Another way is possible. *International Review of Qualitative Research.*

James McNinch
Faculty of Education
University of Regina
Saskatchewan, Canada

JACQUELINE MULDOON

12. CHALLENGE AND COMPLEXITY IN LANDSCAPES OF CHANGE

Building Effective Partnerships

INTRODUCTION

Universities and faculties of education in Ontario now face a changing university environment. In 2013-14 the Ontario government for the first time in history applied policies ("economic levers") to stem the flow of teacher candidates in the Province of Ontario. In 2014 education faculties in universities are still coming to grips with the reality of half the number of teacher candidate spaces, a reduction in BIU funding weightings from 2 to 1.5, and drastic budget cuts. In this changing landscape flexible budgeting, developing and maintaining partnerships, and valuing the knowledge of others is key to survival.

The external environment plays a more dominant role in postsecondary education today than it has in the past. The external pressures of differentiation and Strategic Mandate Agreements compound the internal budgetary pressures within the university system. The dean must not only understand the complex relationships within their own faculty and university but must now pay particular attention to the external environment.

One of the guiding principles within our education faculty is that "effective education is a partnership, where people are valued for their ideas as well as for their participation." This principle is one that has guided me in my Decanal role. Creating working partnerships and valuing those partnerships can enhance relationships both within and external to an organization. Information exchange is enhanced, and honesty and integrity are promoted, which leads to better decision making. Common ground is easier to identify and differences become easier to resolve when partnerships are working effectively and efficiently. It takes strong leadership to create a positive environment and not let negative external forces dictate the issues.

This piece is a reflection on my experience as a dean of education over the past seven years, and the underlying principles that have guided my actions. I explore the central idea that it may sometimes be more effective having a dean from outside the field of education to provide leadership for change.

EFFECTIVE PARTNERSHIPS

Effective partnerships are a shared responsibility in providing opportunities for win-win outcomes. They cannot be versions of zero-sum games where someone benefits at a cost to someone else. These are the types of partnerships that I do my best to promote. Working in partnership, whether it be in our faculty, with our students, district school boards, teaching affiliates, regulatory agencies or government agencies, must be conducted in an environment of respect, trust and shared responsibility. Individuals must be valued for their ideas and points of view as well as for their participation in making decisions. (Dewey, 1938; McCaskell, 2005; Wenger, 1998)

The role of dean is to develop these partnerships (relationships) and guide decision-making both internally and externally. It is important to involve stakeholders in the responsibility for moving toward valued and shared goals. These partnerships will provide an environment that encourages new ideas, questions, and responses. They increase our ability to move forward toward shared goals, even if we have differing ideas on how to get to those goals.

I am, technically, an outsider to education as a discipline. I have a background in the field of mathematics and economics. An odd combination one might think for a dean of education. What can someone from outside the field bring to the position of dean, particularly in this new and complex landscape?

There is no question that the role of any dean has a steep learning curve, and I am still on the upward trajectory. I know that I do not have all the answers, and recognize this may actually be a strength in my role of dean. I listen carefully, ask the right questions and seek the support of those who have the relevant expertise in a wide range of situations. I show my colleagues that I have confidence in their understanding of the field and their judgments on issues. It is this working partnership that allows the achievement of outcomes that are valued to all. I am happy to leave the "Knower's Chair" empty (Maracle 2014). To provide leadership often means leaving this chair empty rather than taking a fixed position. Such a process leads nicely into a shared leadership model as defined by

> the sharing of power and influence among a set of individuals rather than centralizing it in the hands of a single individual who acts as a clear role of dominant superior. (Pearce, Manz, & Sims, 2009, p. 234)

I simply do not possess all the background and information that is needed to make all the decisions—and do not pretend to. My background is only one of many sets of expertise that are necessary in achieving valued and shared goals. Therefore, I am highly dependent on the knowledge of "subject experts." As the dean I can show highly effective leadership in this context by providing solid foundation, vision, positive support and encouragement to build the shared commitment to work towards our goals. This is where I can contribute added value to the decision-making process and outcomes.

GUIDING PRINCIPLES

So what guiding principles can be followed that will encourage and enhance working relationships with the many stakeholders, both within and external to the faculty of education? What platform can be used where information is exchanged with integrity, and where experiences and views of others are valued?

When I first became involved with the School of Education and Professional Learning, I looked carefully at the conceptual framework and guiding principles upon which the School was based (Trent University School of Education and Professional Learning, 2011). It is these guiding principles that allowed me to understand the pedagogy underlying the Bachelor Education program and a commitment to these principles allowed me the opportunity to provide effective leadership. Understanding the value of these principles enables me to be a "supportive coach" (Morgeson, 2005; Carson, Tesluk, & Marrone, 2007). I engage in actions that are supportive of our mandate and vision and encourage the expertise and skills of my faculty. For example, I have encouraged them to take ownership and become leaders themselves; I have provided guidance on specific strategies and directions that help ensure that the activities of the group are aligned with the tasks at hand.

Although our guiding principles are written specifically for teaching and learning in our pre-service and in-service programs I believe they are equally transferable to the formation and maintenance of effective partnerships. For example, a social constructivist approach focuses on an individual's learning that takes place as a result of their interaction in a group (Young & Collin, 2004). The use of critical pedagogy assists in promoting values such as fairness, equity and social justice. Wink (2005, p. 165) points out

> critical pedagogy challenges our long-held assumptions and leads us to as new questions ... change is often difficult, and critical pedagogy is all about change from coercive to collaborative; from transmission to transformative; from inert to catalytic; from passive to active.

In recognizing the differences in the backgrounds of individuals and valuing their assets, we can forward principles of fairness, equity and social justice. Working in partnership, valuing the contributions of others, we are able to mitigate the boundaries that have resulted from past educational practices.

If individuals construct an understanding of experience together, all members of the partnership are valued for their experiences and assets, and everyone is fully engaged in the process, we have shared responsibility for, and ownership of, all decisions. We will have respected the assets and diversity of others. This respect for the assets and diversity of others allows us to work more effectively in achieving our goals and make fair and equitable decisions.

The use of critical pedagogy builds the skills needed for teaching, learning and engaging in the issues in a 21st century environment. Creative and critical thinking, critical reflection, critical engagement and communications (Trilling & Fadel, 2009) enable us, as leaders, to improve our understanding and critically question what has previously been assumed. What would be different if we used a different set of assumptions? We profess to want these skills in our students and we should also strive to make them inherent in our own decision-making processes. We can all benefit by fostering these skills in our partnerships and by using these skills as we make decisions.

These skills of course are not new but rather are skills that are typically embedded in the DNA of a strong liberal arts and science education. What is different today is our increased ability to collect, to use, and to disseminate knowledge and information due to increased use of technology. Improved technology and increased access to a global community is now in our hands (Trilling & Fadel, 2009) and accompanying this must be the openness to accept and appreciate the diversity and assets of individuals.

Educational programming must change to meet a changing world market, with the important caveat that we must be careful not to jump on passing fads. We need to equip all students with the knowledge, skills, and sense of community that will lead to innovation and creativity. Through strong skills in communication, critical thinking and collaboration we can provide opportunities for all to become positive "change agents" in society. We must produce graduates who are adaptable, who are good citizens, and who have strong principles of equity and social justice.

CHANGING EXTERNAL ENVIRONMENT

It is the changing external environment that brings with it increased pressures. It is my observation that the external environment is playing a much more dominant role today than it has in the past. There is a strong potential for the external forces to create increased pressure on decision making. With fewer resources available, fewer students and fewer dollars there is increasing pressure to do more with less. As we adjust to the reality of half the number of teacher candidate spaces, a reduction in BIU funding weights from 2 to 1.5, along with the demand for enhanced content of pre-service programs we struggle with the conflicts this creates with our goals for high quality and academic excellence. How can we do more for less while preserving high quality programming, promote innovation and creativity? Shrinking resources and increased pressure on university budgets and the calls for differentiation and program prioritization make internal decision making difficult. Boards and senior university administration are alarmed by the cuts and the new demands. This trend often deters organizations from thinking outside the box. The ability to innovate, to grow in new directions is compromised. Is there still sufficient room for innovation when the resource constraints seem so overwhelming? Effective partnerships offer a way to guide us through these frequently conflicting pressures and challenges.

For example, the 2014 cuts to education funding and spaces in Ontario provide significant challenges, so much so, that it is difficult to see what opportunities these cuts might also provide. The financial pressures facing the universities lead to direct conflicts when trying to implement enhanced programming. The senior administration and Board are concerned over lost tuition and government grants and how that might affect the institution as a whole. The faculty of education are worried about the reduction in their budgets and the viability of its programs. The external environment (the Ministry of Education and the Ontario College of Teachers) is calling for enhanced and longer programs and more practicum days. Clearly these are agendas that do not align well with each other.

Faced with these demands it was necessary for our tenure-track faculty, as the curriculum leaders, to work effectively in partnership with each other, our university and the external organizations in order to achieve strong outcomes and solutions. When faced with restructuring, we started to dream. After all, the rhetoric we heard was it was an opportunity to provide an enhanced program of study. It was easy to get caught in the trap of "let's do everything." We spent numerous meetings in this stage and it soon became clear that we were having difficulty hearing each other and were failing to recognize the financial constraints that we faced.

At this point I tried a collaborative partnership model to help our planning. Acting as a supportive coach, I provided a timeline and task list that would help us through the planning process. I used my expertise and knowledge of efficiency and finance to provide a clear understanding of the financial constraints facing both our program and the university. I helped redefine our goals from that of the individual to the collective, and offered suggestions on how we might move forward. Discussions then became more realistic. Throughout the discussions I listened to all the voices at the table and respected their experiences and expertise. In fact, in a safe environment of trust and respect, everyone at the table listened and respected the points of view of others. Discussions became organized and more productive.

During the discussions we were able to establish as a starting point that we already had an excellent program and could in fact build upon it. Recognizing the financial constraints and the implications of those constraints for us both as a faculty, and for the institution as a whole, it was our responsibility to solve the problems. And it was a shared responsibility. While there were many opinions on how best to restructure, by working together in partnership a draft structure was complete. In the end faculty felt increased ownership and responsibility for their path forward. Of course, the task does not end there, we are continuing to work in partnership with our entire faculty, other units within the institution, our partner district school boards and the union affiliates to implement our new structure. Although it is always tempting to address our own individual interests, through this process of partnership, we exhibited good citizenship and assumed shared responsibility for the leadership role.

CONCLUSION

This model of shared/collaborative leadership worked well for us. It created an environment of trust and respect where individuals shared their expertise and were valued for that expertise. The ultimate gain was an increased commitment by all for the decisions made. There is better understanding of the decisions (and decision-making processes), clearer communications and more transparency.

Effective partnerships are a practice that works well and can be used with both internal and external partners.

REFERENCES

Carson, J. Tesluk, P. E., & Marrone, J. A. (2007). Shared leadership in teams: An investigation on antecedent conditions and performance. *Academy of Management Journal, 50*, 1217-1234.
Dewey, J. (1938). *Experience and education*. New York, NY: Touchstone.
Maracle, L. (2014, February). *Using Aboriginal teaching and themes to inform our thinking about preparing beginning teachers*. Keynote presentation at the 2014 OTF/OADE Conference, Creating Circles of Hope in Teacher Education, York University, Toronto, ON.
McCaskell, T. (2005). *Race to equity: Disrupting educational inequity*. Toronto, ON: Between the Lines.
Morgeson, F. P. (2005). The external leadership of self-managed teams: Intervening in the context of novel and disruptive events. *Journal of Applied Psychology, 90*, 497-508.
Pearce, C. L., Manz, C. C., & Sims, H. P. Jr. (2009). Where do we go from here?: Is shared leadership the key to team success? *Organizational Dynamics, 38*, 234-238.
Trent University School of Education and Professional Learning (2011). *Conceptual framework*. Retrieved from http://www.trentu.ca/education/faculty/overview_concept.php
Trilling, B., & Fadel, C. (2009). *21st century skills: Learning for life in our times*. San Francisco, CA: Jossey-Bass.
Wenger, E. (1998). *Communities of practice: Learning, meaning, and identity*. Cambridge, UK: Cambridge University Press.
Wink, J. (2005). *Critical pedagogy: Notes from the real world* (3rd ed.). Boston: Pearson/Allyn and Bacon.
Young, R., & Collin, A. (2004). Introduction: Constructivism and social constructionism in the career field. *Journal of Vocational Behaviour, 64*, 373-388.

Jacqueline Muldoon
School of Education and Professional Learning
Trent University
Ontario, Canada

KAREN ROLAND

13. LEADING FROM WITHIN

INTRODUCTION

Changes to teacher education in Ontario have been discussed by political parties over the years; however, the political landscape in the spring of 2013 proved to be the fertile ground required for the government to move forward with this mission. Benjamin Franklin may have warned that death and taxes are certainties, but I would suggest that in the 21st century, change is also a certainty for the academy. Universities today exist in a period of financial exigency, demographic shifts, and the call for institutional differentiation; teacher education is a microcosm within the larger institutional change context.

CHANGES TO TEACHER EDUCATION IN ONTARIO

Driven by the need to address an over-supply of qualified teachers in the province by cutting the number of Bachelor of Education graduates from 9000 to 4500 annually, the Ontario Ministries of Training Colleges and Universities, and Education, instituted provincially mandated changes to teacher education in 2013 which involved: enrolment and graduation caps, a requirement that teacher education programs be expanded from two to four semesters, and the announcement of significant reductions to university funding for students enrolled in Bachelor of Education programs. Institutional Quality Assurance Processes (IQAP) required that faculties of education respond to these programmatic changes within a very challenging timeframe, and also within the context of an institutional differentiation framework. Interestingly, the convergence of these challenges may have actually worked to promote a climate conducive to preparing the faculty to embrace the need for change, and to do so using an institutional lens. Cross-subsidization of programming within the institution, and territorial "differentiation" mindsets, have clarified the need amongst the professoriate, for transformative change, and a focus at the institutional level on teaching and learning as foundational components for all institutional programming. In temporizing teacher education change within the institutional context, questions have arisen about the plight/survival of teacher education programs, or, whether or not the need for change is a duality of both survival as well as enrichment. I would suggest that this duality essentially provided a catalyst with which faculty was able to embrace change and too move forward: on the one hand the changes required to our teacher education program were provincially mandated, including the timelines; and yet, I

S.E. Elliott-Johns (ed.), Leadership for Change in Teacher Education, 87–93.
© 2015 Sense Publishers. All rights reserved.

also believe that meeting these requirements for change provided an opportunity to transform our curriculum, to re-envision teacher education.

Fullan states that, "Probably the two greatest failures of leaders are indecisiveness in times of urgent need for action and dead certainty that they are right in times of complexity" (2008, p. 6). Being aware of this, as the dean, I embarked on this transformative journey, at a programmatic, faculty and institutional level, with the understanding that the nature of my first step in the process would likely set the tone for the consultative process. I decided that active collaboration and engagement in a consultative process was the best way to proceed given the magnitude of the changes required for the teacher education program. Therefore, the first step taken was to convene an Ad Hoc Steering Committee for Teacher Education Change comprised of tenured faculty representing diverse subject areas, and at each of the divisional levels (i.e., Primary/Junior; Junior/Intermediate; and, Intermediate/Senior). This step was taken to effectively begin leading from within.

Consultation—Working Toward Consensus

In preparing for the initial steering committee meeting it was necessary to consider the goals and objectives of this collaboration, and how to best succeed at engaging faculty colleagues in the change process. A routine exercise such as proposing the agenda for the initial meeting required careful consideration of how to go about identifying the issues, as well as potential pathways that might assist the faculty with its development of a framework for the two-year teacher education program (to be implemented by September 2015). This collaborative consultation model was undertaken with the goal to engage faculty in active discussions about change, and to create a communication network comprised of the steering committee members as agents of change, actively facilitating a faculty-wide engagement in the change process. Complex and detailed information to provide a "big picture" perspective was first shared amongst the members of the steering community, and then disseminated to all faculty through this communication network. This layered collaborative consultation model was used as a method to engage colleagues in discussions and to gather the various perspectives from all levels of faculty.

In my leadership role, I took great care during the initial steering committee meetings to present a case concerning the immediacy of the need for change, and the opportunity this change could provide the faculty of education in terms of transforming our teacher education program. For example, one of our first steering committee meetings focused on creating a conceptual map or framework for the new program—our goal from the outset was to transform and enrich our teacher education program, not simply to expand it by two semesters. The framework selected was a four semester program over two years, each year comprised of a fall and winter semester. Additionally, and most importantly, the conceptual framework evolved and included the following themes: Semester 1 theme (Fall Year 1)—Pedagogy, Theories of Teaching & Learning; Semester 2 theme (Winter Year 1)—Theory in Practice; Semester 3 theme (Fall Year 2)—Social, Global and

Cultural Contexts of Education; and, Semester 4 theme (Winter Year 2)—Independent and Reflective Practice. While time consuming, using this collaborative and transparent consultative approach was effective at engaging faculty members, as agents of change, to facilitate change from within by freeing the faculty of education from the confines of the past, and assisting the collective to move beyond the entrenchment of "how things have always been done." This process allowed the faculty, as an engaged collective, to move forward as we re-imagined our work as teacher educators, and in doing so, this freedom in and of itself became "a powerful tool for change" (Fullan, 2011).

The changes facing Ontario faculties of education were driven through top-down mandates (Ministry) and bottom-up forces (intra-faculty consultation) (Hargreaves & Fullan, 2012). The collaborative consultation model was ultimately quite successful regarding the overall conception and focus of the two-year program framework developed. Once developed, it was evident that the framework for the new two-year Bachelor of Education program designed by faculty (within six months, which in itself was quite an accomplishment!), fully embraced and actualized a 21st Century vision of education. In my opinion, this vision of education supports a multi-epistemic approach to the ways of knowing, respect for the impact of lived experience on ontological perspectives, and placing high value on the reciprocity of learning. It was also evident that the new program clearly supported the faculty's mission which states that all of our undertakings are guided and shaped by a commitment to equity and social justice in education. This commitment was evident through the inclusion of service learning as a foundational aspect of the program. As as an experiential learning strategy, service learning provides teacher candidates with the opportunity to connect theory and pedagogy in community-based learning experiences. By linking classroom theory with direct experience and engagement within the local and global communities, we hope to foster civic responsibility and engagement.

The foundational aspects of the new two-year program clearly aligned with stated learning outcomes for graduates, including: civic engagement, belief in the reciprocity of learning, and a reflective appreciation and value for multi-epistemic perspectives about knowledge. I attribute this success to what Hargreaves and Fullan term as, "subsidiarity" (2012, p. 175), the practice of ensuring that individuals who are facilitators of change, are enabled and supported in decision making and connecting them in a manner to create coherence in messaging and delivery, and to work toward consensus. My leadership during this process, the goal of which was to consult to create consensus in the transformation of our teacher education program, required a tenuous balancing of guidance with informative direction: guiding faculty by linking incremental changes to create a gestalt-perspective of the program framework, and providing information to direct our progress as we collectively navigated the benchmarks and goals identified as critical to the transformative process.

However, the consultative model was less successful in terms of combating subject-specific balkanization. Balkanization arose during final discussions around subject specific allocations of time within the two-year program schedule.

Hargreaves and Fullan purport that "collaborative cultures don't railroad other people's agendas and purposes" (2012, p. 113), and so it was necessary for me in facilitating and leading the change process to not only create the space for open and respectful dialogue, but also to ensure that the momentum for change was not lost. Therefore, when these issues came to the fore, as the dean, I engaged faculty in these courageous and difficult conversations, with the understanding that consensus may not always be a satisfying outcome. Ultimately, the faculty reached consensus in developing a unique and innovative framework for the transformation and enrichment of its two-year teacher education program. During this change process I felt that the best method to assist us collectively in steering through the (at times) turbulent and challenging terrain was, as the leader, to remain focused on the original program goals identified at the beginning of the consultation. This was accomplished through the continual and clear messaging and interpretation of these goals, maintaining civility and collegiality during what were at times difficult conversations, and keeping at the forefront the fact that consensus requires give and take, but ultimately is beneficial to our work in transforming the Bachelor of Education program.

I have reflected on some of the guideposts that directed this journey of transformative change for the faculty; the guideposts that proved to be most helpful with successfully facilitating change included: 1) careful selection of members from the larger faculty group to create a steering committee comprised of individuals who had the capacity to become *change agents*, and by this I mean, those visionaries who had the capacity to break "their own mold" (Hargreaves & Fullan, 2012, p. 174) to enact change; 2) in an effort to contextualize the changes required for teacher education relative to the broader institutional differentiation framework, it was necessary for me to create the first "sketch of the big picture" and to consistently communicate this information, particularly as the sketch evolved through the consultation process; 3) another key aspect in successfully navigating change was to ensure a steady momentum toward achieving our goal—this was accomplished by constantly updating our planning timeline and noting achievements and issues for discussion; 4) and finally, being a reflexive leader, was essential—reflexivity, the awareness and intrapersonal knowledge of the impact my leadership would have on the change process was required. With regard to reflexivity, Luttrell (2000) suggests that:

> We listen and make sense of what we hear according to particular theoretical, ontological, personal, and cultural frameworks and in the context of unequal power relations. The worry always exists that the voices and perspectives of those we study [and in this case, consult and collaborative with] will be lost or subsumed to our own views and interest. (p. 499)

Enacting Transformative Change

As dean, I found that it was essential to recognize the importance of the three C's to enacting transformative change (Hargreaves & Fullan, 2012): capability to do the work; credibility to engender trust (particularly important for the leader); and, connectedness—ensuring collective support through the consistency of messaging and the accessibility of the members of the steering committee. It is my opinion that working as a community of practice the faculty of education was able to navigate the challenges created by this climate of change through actively sharing their personal experiences, their knowledge, and their vision of teacher education, in a collaborative and consultative manner, which ultimately lead to consensus-driven decisions.

As the dean of an Ontario faculty of education, I anticipate, and welcome, the occasions that are surely to arise as the importance of education, and educators, endures to address the opportunities and challenges created by our multicultural and globalized societies.

REFERENCES

Fullan, M. (2008). *The six secrets of change: What the best leaders do to help their organizations survive and thrive.* San Francisco, CA: Jossey-Bass.

Fullan, M. (2011). *Change leader: Learning to do what matters most.* San Francisco, CA: Jossey-Bass.

Hargreaves, A., & Fullan, M. (2012). *Professional capital: Transforming teaching in every school.* Toronto, ON: Ontario Principals' Council.

Luttrell, W. (2000). Good enough methods for ethnographic research. *Harvard Educational Review, 70,* 499-524. Retrieved from: http://www.indiana.edu/~educy520/sec5982/week_5/luttrell00.pdf

Karen Roland
Faculty of Education
University of Windsor
Ontario, Canada

ANN SHERMAN

14. TEACHER EDUCATOR AND DEAN

Challenges, Joys, Trials and Successes

INTRODUCTION

As a dean of a faculty of education, there are many challenges and joys, trials and success. Perhaps the best thing about being in a faculty of education is working with a group of professors who are committed to providing the best possible teacher education program to our pre-service teachers. Our students are, for the most part, eager to be teachers who inspire their own students to become curious and engaged learners. So I am constantly asking myself, as a teacher educator and dean, how do I help my colleagues create an environment where we are inspiring our pre-service teachers to be curious and engaged learners?

THE CHALLENGE

I lay awake at night wondering if we have provided enough knowledge, prompting and support to give our beginning teachers the courage and backbone to go out into public schools and work both with and against what they find there. I often say that the problem with school is that we all went there. By that I mean that all of us who have attended school…teachers, students, parents, and members of the public all have experiences with the performance part of teaching. We all know what classrooms were like for us, and our opinions of what school should be like is influenced by those experiences. This is supported by the work of Lortie (2002). We come to teacher education with pre-formed ideas of what makes learning appropriate, exciting, or professional. But few of our pre-service teachers enter the teacher education program knowing what happens prior to the teacher stepping into the classroom. Certainly they recognize that teachers come prepared. They can see that teachers have photocopied something, or created a power point presentation, they have arranged the desks in a certain way and they have a plan for how the day might go.

Many of our pre-service teachers are quite good at some of the performance aspects of teaching. They have experience working with children, they have coached, or tutored, or taught private lessons in piano or swimming, to name a few. But what keeps me awake at night is the worry that we don't have the time or opportunity to help these beginning teachers truly develop a theoretical framework that can provide an underpinning for their own teaching. Many would argue that it will take years of practice to truly develop philosophical and theoretical understanding that are foundational to the way we engage learners. But with our limited time frame of the Bachelor of Education degree, we do need to think about and commit to ways of providing the best opportunities for our pre-service teachers to engage in discussions that raise awareness of philosophies and theories about learning, (and) as well as the time to put into practice strategies that are based on these same philosophies and theories.

As more and more degrees are truncated in terms of time, we find ourselves looking for ways to combine, collaborate and integrate the kinds of thinking and learning we want to, and can provide, for our B.Ed. students. But it is challenging. Our university offers a 60-credit, post-graduate degree as a Bachelor of Education and we do this in 11 months. This means the pre-service teachers are in our classrooms four days a week and in public schools one day a week, other than 12 other weeks of intense classroom practicum. The days are long and the work is intense and yet we still struggle to provide opportunities for B.Ed. students to experience exposure to the many ideas with which we feel it is important for them to become familiar.

We experiment with our timetable, with our courses, with who teaches for how long. We get a great deal of student feedback as well as feedback from cooperating teachers, Ministry of Education personnel and school superintendents. And, the data tells us, we are doing a good job.

But what is still missing? There is little research about Canadian teacher education programs and we have had little experience in Canada finding ways to assess our success in preparing teachers. There is data that shows that teachers sometimes do not stay after their first five years (Alberta Education, 2012), and other deans of education across Canada describe how many of their teacher education programs are struggling to meet admission quotas as fewer teachers are being hired across the nation. But what do we really know about what makes teacher education programs successful?

THE LEADERSHIP PROCESS

As a dean, I have searched for ways to facilitate deep and meaningful discussions about our mission and desires for our student teachers. We continue to ask whether, how, and to what extent, emphasis is given to ensuring pre-service teachers are supported in developing their own clearly articulated and grounded theoretical framework to guide their professional decision-making (Brouwer & Korthagen, 2005).

Our focus, as a faculty, has been on the uncovering of beginning teachers' embedded understandings, providing experiences that enable the creation of their theoretical lenses, and then establish opportunities for them to re-experience school in ways that modify, update, and even replace historical individual and societal perceptions of schools. The "care-full" integration of understandings through reflective practice can, over time, lead to what Trotman and Kerr (2001) refer to as a "perspective transformation." We believe that teacher educators must deliberately create opportunities for these transformations through the creation of a dissonance in the pre-service teachers' thinking about preconceptions and assumptions they bring with them. We believe it is through emerging self-awareness and theoretical understanding that clarity of practice is situated and can develop further. For example, we are attempting to create a holistic teacher education framework which will situate critical reflection and application as integral to pre-service teachers' experiences and we are working to demonstrate that these are best facilitated through carefully crafted school-university-government collaborations.

Our stakeholders outside of the university (e.g. school districts, provincial department of education) are extremely important to our success and we work deliberately to collaborate, support and educate others about our hopes and intentions. As the dean, I am asked to interact with the superintendents, the government representatives, school teachers, other deans across Canada and it is important to enable linkages between all of these groups to find ways to create the opportunities for pre-service teachers to meet their own expectations and the expectations of all these stakeholder groups. So to say a dean must be able to handle multiple perspectives is an understatement. Numerous perspectives must be juggled and remember, this is where "the trouble with school is that everyone went there" philosophy is particularly important. As I meet these various representatives, I can't help but notice how often people refer back to their own school day experiences. Even those who are well educated and knowledgeable about learning, education and schooling (and their differences) refer back to their own school experiences. I, myself, refer fondly to Mrs. Rose, my Grade 3-4 teacher who took us for scientific walks to a local lake and had us create artwork with some of the objects of nature we collected, once the science experiments were finished.

So it takes a certain political astuteness to be a dean who can inform others and provide the kind of leadership needed to change education today. Many issues around teacher preparation can also be seen as opportunities for discussion and learning and we need to continue to find ways to draw all other stakeholders into continuous discussion. The kind of teacher education program I described earlier has many supporters as well as detractors. Some think pre-service teachers should spend more time learning classroom discipline than I do. Others think they should have less time at the university and more time in school classrooms. Some are small disagreement and others are larger and more philosophically based.

I see these tensions, and sometimes mismatched purposes, as opportunities to educate others in a very mindful and purposeful manner. Canadian author Gilles Paquet (2009) describes a process he calls "scheming virtuously." He says his idea is a call to active engagement, imaginative problem solving and reframing of organizational design for effective action through the creation appreciative systems. Faculty colleagues in education, are placed in a position where we can ask ourselves how our relationships with educational stakeholders can disrupt their beliefs, policies, values and assumptions. As the dean, I am in a position to problematize and ask questions that shake up and reconstruct understandings about public schooling and the ways that teacher education programs can help support transformational change in schools.

Furthermore, as a dean of a faculty of education, I find myself in a position where I can help create and facilitate a process somewhat similar to Paquet's notion of scheming virtuously—within and outside of our faculty. I seek to do this explicitly and intentionally as we plan for collaboration and the sharing of knowledge. As a faculty we are seeking a care-full way of engaging others so that we all share knowledge and come to better understand our own power in the situation and recognize whose voices are overpowering others. This process has also demonstrated the need to explicitly acknowledge the importance of tone, clarity and intention in all communication with other stakeholders. As the dean, I must acknowledge that we need to be both supportive and subversive as we seek ways to influence how decisions are made. We recognize that power can change the way people address issues, that a lack of knowledge can be a terrifying thing in the hands of someone with power but no knowledge, and that many people base their decisions about what is appropriate for beginning teachers on their own experience of school, and yet don't always realize this.

The politics of care insists that we exist with others through an open sharing of what we know in a mindful way. Disagreements occur, but every step we take with our colleagues is thought out in a way that follows the very principles we believe all learners deserve: For example, the opportunity to build on what they already know, and to experience new learnings in caring environments in a respectful and encouraging way. As we build new and innovative ways to engage our pre-service teachers we understand that our decisions impact more than the students in our B.Ed. program. Changes to our teacher education program have far reaching impacts on many people. As dean, I work to provide the leadership to ensure the processes we put in place help us all work towards the most appropriate experiences for our pre-service teachers to benefit their future students in schools.

REFERENCES

Alberta Education. (2012). *A transformation in progress: Alberta's ECS-12 Education Workforce 2011/2012*. Edmonton: Alberta Education.

Brouwer, N., & Korthagen, F. (2005). Can teacher education make a difference? *American Educational Research Journal, 42*, 153-224.

Lortie, D. C. (2002). *Schoolteacher* (2nd ed.). Chicago, IL: University of Chicago Press.

Paquet, G. (2009). *Scheming virtuously: The road to collaborative governance*. Ottawa, ON: Invenire Books.

Trotman, J., & Kerr, T. (2001). Making the personal professional: Pre-service teacher education and personal histories. *Teachers and Teaching: Theory and Practice, 7*, 157-171.

Ann Sherman
Faculty of Education
University of New Brunswick
New Brunswick, Canada

SUSAN E. ELLIOTT-JOHNS

CODA

Insights Gleaned from the Voices of Deans of Education

This project sought to explore insights and multiple perspectives on leading for change in teacher education by inviting deans of education across Canada to share their lived experiences in the current era of teacher education reform. The fourteen essays by contributing authors offer increased understandings of the nature of their work in the context of significant transitions, complexity, change, and uncertainties.

Evidently, there is much to be learned by listening to the voices of these deans of education. Change is a dynamic and, at times, can be a very difficult process (Malone, 2013). The tendency to gravitate towards existing practices, patterns of behaviour, and familiar expectations when working through processes of change is not unusual and we often "perceive externally driven change as a directive, an imposition, an intrusion, and a disruption to our daily work" (Malone, p. 128). Such factors do not always facilitate processes of change. Perceptions of imposition and intrusion appear to be as much the case for deans of education and teacher educators today as for those educators employed in school systems, in Canada and beyond (and, equally, for the many other stakeholders in post-secondary education currently navigating complex processes of change, educational reform, fiscal restraint, and uncertainty around the world).

Alternatively, change tends to occur more easily when it is co-constructed, meaningful and purposeful, in line with our values and beliefs, and when the potential for change is perceived to genuinely improve existing conditions:

> positive change flourishes in in environments that are inspiring and inclusive, that negotiate internal and external expectations, and that empower all stakeholders along a path towards shared goals and outcomes. (Fullan, 2011, as cited in Malone, 2013, p. 128)

The authentic voices of fourteen deans of education gathered in this unique collection of essays offer valuable insights into the challenges and processes of leadership for change currently evolving in faculties of education across Canada. There is something compelling about studying the every day, commonplace lived experience that can reveal much about who we are, our attitudes and values, and approaches to our work. Not surprisingly perhaps, critical issues resonating through these reflections emphasize approaches to social justice in teacher education (including broad understandings of the importance of Indigenous teacher education), approaches to effective leadership in contemporary contexts and perspectives on the need to retain focus on the "bigger picture" (or vision) for teacher education. Three clearly interconnected themes reflecting perspectives on leadership for change in teacher education surface consistently in and across these deans' essays: 1) The centrality of people and relationships; 2) Understanding new approaches to teaching, learning, and teacher education and 3) Complexities inherent in "leading the change." Each of the three themes will be discussed, followed by recommendations for further research and practice.

CENTRALITY OF PEOPLE AND THE BUILDING OF EFFECTIVE RELATIONSHIPS

Consistent with Gmelch (2002) and recurring references to the need for teamwork, patience, balance and personal sacrifice in the dean's role, the essays in this volume describe authors' perceptions of leadership as, first and foremost, about people and the building and sustaining of effective relationships with a diverse range of personnel across multifaceted contexts. Successful relationships were consistently cited as vital to resilience and renewal for individuals and their organizations. Lewis, for example, sees teaching and leadership as inextricably linked and argues that both constructs are essentially about people and relationships. Subthemes recurring across many of the essays included the importance of building trust, explicit understandings of organizational culture when seeking to bring about change, and the need for sustained, positive interactions in the building of trust in administrative leadership (e.g., Duncan).

As deans, both Muldoon and Roland describe having attempted to promote "shared leadership," highlighting the need not only for skilled leadership but an attitudinal orientation to forging and sustaining effective working partnerships. They cite shared commitment for working towards identified goals, shared responsibilities for moving forward, and concerted efforts to create spaces for respectful dialogue and consensus as partially responsible for success in leading their faculty (specifically, for example, in recent program restructuring processes at their respective institutions).

Education is a provincial responsibility in Canada. Opinions about education continue to come from many sides and from many self-appointed experts across local and provincial jurisdictions within individual provinces, as well as in dialogue across the country. The difficulties these deans of education describe facing as they attempt to navigate political waters successfully—sometimes beginning with the internal task of building relationships with a wide range of faculty and staff holding very disparate views—can undoubtedly make the building of trust in administrative leadership a highly complex endeavour. Leadership qualities of deans of education might well be considered as situational, rather than unequivocally universal. Andersen (2002) summarized it this way,

> Each dean's position is truly unique because of the local campus culture, the organizational structure, compatibility of leaders' and followers' styles, and attending circumstances .... The expectations that a wide range of publics have for the role of the dean ... and other immediate considerations are never quite the same from place to place. (p. 106)

In a climate of rapidly changing educational environments, Roland's focus on a "consultative" approach to leadership suggests a starting point that clearly resonates with the theme of building relationships. Beginning with a belief in change as certainty for the academy in the 21C, her work is informed by Fullan's (2008) perspective, "Probably the two greatest failures of leaders are indecisiveness in times of urgent need for action, and dead certainty that they are right in times of complexity." Roland's insights into the pros and cons of consultative leadership as effective leadership for change in contemporary teacher education (e.g., subject-specific "balkanization" still prevalent and difficult to change) highlight the importance of skilled leadership and the ability to build effective relationships in support of change in contemporary teacher education.

UNDERSTANDING NEW APPROACHES TO TEACHING, LEARNING, AND TEACHER EDUCATION

While rapid and recent changes in approaches to teaching and learning in global school systems are well documented (Hargreaves & Shirley, 2012), changes in faculties of education have not received nearly as much attention. That said, changes in approaches to teaching and learning have had an enormous impact on the work of deans of education and their respective teacher education programs— programs of study designed to prepare professionals for success in the field of teaching:

> Leading a productive school, college, or department of education has always been a challenge. Teacher education, for example, has been under constant criticism for 20 years. Deans, consequently, are often the focus of those who want change and they want it now. Teaching has become a public act open to inspection by everyone interested in any aspect of what happens in PK-12 schools or colleges and universities. (Glenn, 2002, p. 8)

However, the intense scrutiny of teacher education in general and the design, content, and organization of teacher education programs in particular, continues to increase (seemingly, exponentially). How deans of education, and teacher educators, prepare teachers has indeed, it seems, become everyone's business. For example, Mandzuk cites Tom (1997) when suggesting, "in many ways, everyone is in charge of teacher education, yet nobody is."

Khalideen emphasizes the seismic shift encountered by deans "as academic leaders and middle managers" as they work to successfully navigate the many competing agendas that pull in very different directions. Characteristics of effective leadership were also described as attention to sustaining what is working well and processes of continuous improvement—also seen as equally vital in current teacher education practice, increasing complexities, and calls for change (Franklin).

Magnusson reminds us that teacher education programs across Canada were developed, for the most part, to maximize educational impact within the constraints of university structures—these structures also having been designed for other purposes and other times. He asks, "How do we bring new attitudes, ideas, and practices into our places of learning?" and argues the advent of new technologies offer opportunities to think very differently about teacher education. However, exchanging comfortable structures and assumptions from past practice for beliefs and practices associated with innovative teaching and learning also requires highly skilled leadership. The Native Teacher Education Program (NTEP) located in the Yukon is in, "a unique context for Indigenous education in Canada," and Bartlette's essay focuses on increased understandings of the importance of promoting critical pedagogy and rigorous self-reflection in teacher education for Indigenous and non-Indigenous teachers. Finally, Sherman suggests deans are in a position, should they choose, "to problematize and ask questions that shake up and reconstruct understandings about ... the ways that teacher education programs can support transformational change in schools."

Reflections in these essays not only draw our attention to the critical role of deans of education in provoking, supporting and championing new ideas and approaches to pedagogy for contemporary teacher education; they suggest various ways proactive leadership for change in teacher education might also be a catalyst for transformation and change in schools.

COMPLEXITIES INHERENT IN LEADING THE CHANGE

The multiple, and multi-faceted, complexities experienced in leading change are reflected in all of the essays contributed by deans of education. This project enabled the sharing of unique "insider stories" and different perspectives on the topic from deans across the country. The deans' voices also draw attention to some of the socio-cultural factors relevant to teacher education in situated contexts as well as some of the specific complexities encountered. Table 1 presents a sampling of frequently recurring examples of external/internal conditions and inherent tensions described across several essays. Andersen (2002) writes, "Education has become a political football that easily lends itself to varying positions and demands of vested interest groups, differing philosophies of government, and disparate visions of the future" (p. 101). Instances of navigating the increasingly complex and competing agendas that are teacher education today recur over and again in the deans' reflections. Working effectively with many different stakeholders (internally and externally) on issues related to teaching and learning, heightens awareness of the need for deans to understand new approaches to teaching, learning, and leading in faculties of education, expressly as leaders of change in programs of teacher education.

Mandzuk cites the increasing emphasis on external relations with, for example, government and the media, and "development work" (a.k.a. fundraising). He highlights the vital role for the dean in capacity building and succession planning and, while pointing out the challenging aspects of developing leadership capacity within faculties, Mandzuk also clarifies why he regards it as such an important dimension of his work.

Table 1. *Complexities in leading the change: External/internal conditions and inherent tensions frequently identified by deans of education*

BUILDING/ SUSTAINING RELATIONSHIPS:	Bringing internal and external communities together e.g., inner city location of campus and impact of/ response to issues	Finding ways to balance internal (institutional) pressures with external (multiple stakeholders and turbulent times)	Dean as a member of the Senior (Executive) Team as well as advocating for faculty (dual agendas that do not easily co-exist)	Multifaceted landscape of teacher ed. for change, and many "players" involved	How can our relationships with educational stakeholders disrupt their beliefs, policies, values, and assumptions? (As Paquet, 2009 and "scheming virtuously")
SOCIO-POLITICAL-CULTURAL-TEMPORAL COMPLEXITIES:	Engagement in collaborative problem-solving: shared responsibility for charting directions for change	Challenges of time constraints re. development of both theoretical frameworks and effective practice	Approaches to authentic teacher education for social justice? Towards broadening experiences	Towards Indigenous teacher education for all? (i.e., just education systems for Indigenous people and for all?)	Approaches to "leading the change" as a result of mandated circumstances
INTERNAL/ EXTERNAL POLITICS OF CHANGE:	Provincially mandated changes to teacher education (e.g., in Ontario): enrolment and graduation caps, expanded program, significant reductions to funding for students in B.Ed programs	Top-down mandates (OME) and bottom-up forces (intra-faculty consultation)	Impact of government legislated change to publically funded universities, towards policy of differentiation; challenges inherent in the differentiation agenda	Perceived neo-liberal agendas of many governments in Canada today	Policy based regulations vs. guidelines are very different. Regulations and laws demand compliance in practice …

Each of the essays by McNinch, McCluskey, and Cammarata et al. share richly textured glimpses into other significant complexities involved in "leading the change," and insights specific to awareness of, and commitment to, distinct cultural, political, and social context(s) in which their teacher education programs operate. For example, McNinch describes "working against the grain" of powerful neo-liberal rhetoric to challenge erroneous assumptions about teacher education. The articulation of a social justice framework is at the heart of his leadership for change, and he takes serious issue with provincial, national and global agendas that promote positivist, clinical and technical-rational models, preferring more humanist and relational approaches.

McCluskey frames complexities in his leadership as a dean working to mobilize teacher education for social justice—a direct result of the specific location of his university campus. While much continues to be written about social justice as a critical component of programs preparing teachers for contemporary classrooms, what does this really mean? look like? sound like? McCluskey's work offers a list of fifteen guiding principles that illustrate potential approaches to integrating an inner-city context and its related issues directly into a teacher education program.

In their essay (presented here in both official languages of Canada, French and English), Cammarata, Cavanagh, and D'Entremont describe the rationale for and restructuring of a unique teacher education program in a "minority context"—i.e., the only Francophone university campus West of Manitoba where beginning teachers can study, live and socialize in an active Francophone and Francophile community. The navigation of inherent complexities in leadership for change here underscores the prevalence of shared vision and a commitment to democratic processes.

Albert Einstein once said, "We cannot solve the problems that we have created with the same thinking that created them." The contributors of these essays clearly demonstrate commitment to teacher education leadership, with all its challenges and complexities, and to enacting different ways of thinking about (and resolving) problems encountered in their work.

Beyond formal qualifications and experience, sustaining leadership requires enormous amounts of energy, enthusiasm, depth, breadth and resourcefulness. The essence of the following quotation from *Sustainable Leadership* (Hargreaves & Fink, 2008) resonates throughout these essays, along with its notable cautions in terms of supporting sustainable leadership:

> Leadership isn't and shouldn't be easy. ... It is hard to be a successful leader. It is harder still to be a sustainable one. ... Sustainable educational leaders promote and practice sustaining learning. Sustainable leaders sustain others as they pursue this cause together. Sustainable leaders also sustain themselves, attending to their own renewal and not sacrificing themselves too much as they serve their community. Sustainable leaders stay the course, stay together, stay around, and stay alive. (p. 272)

CODA

CONCLUSIONS AND RECOMMENDATIONS FOR FURTHER RESEARCH

To conclude, the nature of the dean's role is a highly complex balancing act of leadership, administration, and management of academics in situated contexts; it is also a rapidly changing role, internally and externally political, and a role that requires incumbents to serve many masters. Carving out time to maintain research and writing presents yet another challenge, but was something close to the heart of the deans who contributed here. Several are deeply engaged in research on teacher education, pursuing questions of particular interest to them and/or their faculty. For example, explorations of issues in program renewal and social justice—toward relational pedagogy (McNinch); towards flexible, learner-centered teacher education programs with a focus on inquiry and experiential learning (Duncan); designing a holistic teacher education framework—which situates critical reflection and application as integral to pre-service teachers' experiences (Sherman). Pursuit of these research interests contributes further knowledge and understanding deans can bring to their role as leaders of teacher education and their efforts should be encouraged, applauded and supported (internally and externally). As we seek to understand more about Canadian teacher education, and what makes it successful, it is important for deans to encounter frequent opportunities to share their emic perspectives and understandings with other researchers, academic leaders, stakeholders and decision-makers.

Long a champion of teacher education and teacher education research, former dean of education Dr. Peter Grimmett (Simon Fraser University), received the Canadian Association Lifetime Research Achievement Award (2014) from the Canadian Association for Teacher Education (CATE). An excerpt from Grimmett's acceptance speech makes clear his concerns, and voice, as a scholar, researcher, and former dean of teacher education:

> The tradition of teacher education, however, is under attack and needs to be upheld. Teacher education in Canada is like a caged bird: It is attacked within the university, characterized as "domestic labour" by other streams of educational research and non-education disciplinary research (what I'm calling the free birds), it is attacked by policy makers (particularly neo-liberalist ones) who see it as redundant and irrelevant; and yet its researchers sing, they sing about the freedom of preparing teachers as poised, public intellectuals capable of educating today's youth for the vexing problems of tomorrow. (Grimmett, May, 26/2014, at Brock University, Ontario, Canada)

Notably, citing Maya Angelou's poem, "Caged Bird," to characterize teacher education researchers in Canada, Grimmett went on to say, "Teacher education in Canada is like a caged bird: We have to sing about the freedom to make pedagogy trump politics both within our own universities and in society in general."

The processes of leading change described in these deans' essays (and, specifically, engagement in the restructuring of teacher education in the broader context of post-secondary education) portray a leadership role habitually required to navigate something like a metaphor of "permanent white water." Several deans describe work consistent with leading teacher education to where pedagogy trumps politics. But it's an uphill climb! While the commitment to their role as deans is unmistakable the future, as Andersen (2002) concluded, will continue to bring both anticipated and unanticipated challenges; Glenn (2002, p. 8) suggested, "It will not be a calm sea, but it can be an exhilarating ride."

One of the significant and continuing challenges is likely to be effective succession planning and sustainable leadership if a) current leaders are unable to "stay the course, stay together, stay around, and stay alive" (Hargreaves & Fink, 2008, p. 272) and/or b) the pool of candidates willing to take on this demanding role continue to dwindle (see Mandzuk's discussion of the challenges encountered in recruiting deans at the national level and his efforts to continue "identifying, nurturing and supporting potential leaders" at the local level and Khalideen's discussion of the deanship and "Leading in the 21st Century Learning Environment").

Therefore, urgent attention to the preparation of deans and support for their ongoing professional learning and leadership needs to be critically examined in practice and supported in research and practice. The following excerpt from a quotation by Pinnegar and Erickson (2008) appears equally relevant to a call for research that further explores the multiple dimensions of deans' leadership roles, with a view to clarifying the nature of relevant and supportive professional learning:

> We need to continue to explore the relationships between theory, practice, and experience. … How do we and can we marshal theory, practice, experience, and beliefs to develop this terrain in ways that are most constructive for the context in which they are being constructed? (pp. 433-434)

Further research is recommended that explores university-wide (and beyond) understandings of the contemporary role(s) of deans of education, the preparation and training they currently receive, challenges they face in their role, the nuanced balancing acts encountered in their work, and the kinds of ongoing professional learning needed to truly succeed in sustainable leadership for change. There are multiple career pathways to becoming dean and there are many meetings, sessions, seminars and short courses to attend; however, once a dean there appears to be little that explicitly supports sustained professional learning in the dean's role—for example, "no leadership academy for senior leaders but a lot of 'sink or swim' in the murky politics of university life" (K. Anderson, personal communication, March 2, 2014).

Research that offers better understandings, and supports, acknowledges, complements and extends the complex work of deans, is not prevalent in the literature. It is hoped the diverse voices of deans gathered in this unique collection of brief essays, and the insights gleaned from their emic (insider) perspectives on leadership for change in teacher education, will not only contribute to addressing noticeable gaps in the current literature but also provoke discussion and increase interest in related research, research, professional learning, and support for sustainable leadership.

REFERENCES

Andersen, D. G. (2002). The deans of the future. In W.H. Gmelch (Ed.), *Deans' balancing acts: Education leaders and the challenges they face* (p. 106). Washington, DC: American Association of Colleges for Teacher Education.

Bowen, L. S. (Ed.). (1995). (Ed.). *The wizards of odds: Leadership journeys of education deans.* Washington, DC: American Association of Colleges for Teacher Education.

Fullan, M. (2008). *The six secrets of change: What the best leaders do to help their organizations survive and thrive.* San Francisco, CA: Jossey-Bass.

Fullan, M. (2011). *Choosing the wrong drivers for whole system reform.* Centre for Strategic Education Seminar Series Paper, No. 24. Available at www.cse.edu.au

Glenn, A. D. (2002). Foreword. In W. H. Gmelch (Ed.), *Deans' balancing acts: Education leaders and the challenges they face* (p. 8). Washington, DC: American Association of Colleges for Teacher Education.

Gmelch, W. H. (Ed.). (2002). *Deans' balancing acts: Education leaders and the challenges they face.* Washington, DC: American Association of Colleges for Teacher Education.

Grimmett, P. (2014, May). Acceptance Speech on receipt of the 2014 CATE Lifetime Research Achievement Award. Canadian Association for Teacher Education Annual Meeting, Brock University. Retrieved from https.sites.google.com/site/cssecate/awards

Hargreaves, A., & Fink, D. (2008). *Sustainable leadership.* San Francisco, CA: Jossey-Bass.

Hargreaves, A., & Shirley, D. (2012). *The global fourth way: The quest for educational excellence.* Thousand Oaks, CA: Corwin Press.

Malone, H. J. (Ed.). (2013). *Leading educational change: Global issues, challenges, and lessons on whole-system reform.* New York, NY: Teachers College Press.

Pinnegar, S., & Erickson, L. (2008). Using what we know to question what we know about teacher education. In C. Craig & L. R. Deretchin (Eds,), *Imagining a renaissance in teacher education: ATE Yearbook* (pp. 422-436) Lanham, MD: Rowan & Littlefield Education in partnership with the Association of Teacher Educators.

Tom, A. (1997). *Redesigning teacher education.* New York, NY: New York Press.

Susan E. Elliott-Johns
Schulich School of Education
Nipissing University
Ontario, Canada

ABOUT THE CONTRIBUTORS

Deb Bartlette is Vice-President, Academic and Student Services, at Yukon College. She holds an Ed.D from Simon Fraser University, in which she focused on the effect of neo-liberalism on the public good of education and ethics. She feels this was excellent preparation for being a senior administrator. Deb is currently Adjunct Professor of Education with SFU and Visiting Graduate Professor at Athabasca University, teaching courses on social justice and education. Her work at Yukon College includes development of the College's own degrees, including a degree in Indigenous governance and increasing online, blended and condensed programming to improve access to education in the North. The College's B.Ed, the Yukon Native Teacher Education, offered in partnership with the University of Regina, prepares teachers for work in the North by through education and experience with Yukon First Nations and Indigenous history and culture.

Fiona Blaikie is a professor of art education and curriculum, and Dean of the Faculty of Education at Brock University in St. Catharines, Canada. She holds a PhD from the University of British Columbia. Fiona is the former Director of the Joint PhD Program in Educational Studies, and she was deputy chief examiner of visual arts for the International Baccalaureate Organization. She is Past President of the Canadian Society for Education through Art (CSEA), and is a current World Councilor on the Executive of the International Society for Education through Art. Her scholarship has evolved from examining aesthetic values inherent in criteria for assessment to arts-informed research focusing on social theory on the body and clothing. She has won numerous awards including the CSEA Affiliate Award for Ontario for scholarship in arts education as well as Honorary Lifetime Membership of the CSEA.

Laurent Cammarata, Ph.D., is Associate Professor in Education at Faculté Saint-Jean/University of Alberta. He has also been a Summer Lecturer at the University of Minnesota since 2006. Formerly a language teacher, Dr. Cammarata currently works in the preparation and ongoing professional development of K-12 teachers in French immersion and francophone minority settings. His line of research concentrates on exploring means to help novice and veteran teachers become more empowered in their practice through the use of curricular and instructional alternatives such as content-based instruction. Dr. Cammarata's publications have appeared in well-respected scientific venues such as the *Canadian Modern Language Review, Foreign Language Annals, L2 Journal,* and *the Modern Language Journal.* He is also the 2013 recipient of the prestigious "Paul Pimsleur Award for Research in Foreign Language Education," which recognizes outstanding contributions to research in foreign language and second language education.

ABOUT THE CONTRIBUTORS

Martine Cavanagh is professor and head of the Education program at the Faculté Saint-Jean in the University of Alberta. She completed her doctorate in education from the University of Sherbrooke (Quebec) in 2002 specializing in the teaching of writing. For the past 10 years, she has taught courses in the Education program at the Faculty Saint-Jean on literacy teaching and learning at the elementary and secondary levels and conducted research in Francophone schools in Edmonton on teaching the writing of argumentative, expository and narrative texts using a socioconstructivist approach with a focus on writing strategies. Currently, she is conducting a longitudinal study on the teaching of imaginative and realistic story writing to Grade 4 and 5 students. She is also a participant in a research project examining teacher educators' perceptions of the challenges related to the preparation of student teachers in the immersion and Francophone minority contexts.

Yvette d'Entremont is Associate Dean (Academic) and Education Professor at Faculté Saint-Jean/University of Alberta. Her teaching career in mathematics began in 1975 after having completed a BA in mathematics from Mount Saint Vincent University (Halifax, NS) and a B. Ed from Acadia University (Wolfville, NS). Dr. d'Entremont taught high school mathematics in the Francophone schools of Nova Scotia and in Edmonton, Alberta. Upon completion of her doctoral program (University of Alberta), she was recruited to teach mathematics and science methods to education students at Faculté Saint-Jean. She has been an academic staff member at Faculté Saint-Jean since 1990 and has held a number of administrative positions as well as teaching at the undergraduate and the graduate level. Her present research involves the teaching of mathematics through culture. Her most recent presentation on the subject (*Linking Mathematics, Culture and Community*) was at a conference in Paris in June 2014.

Heather Duncan is professor and Dean of Education, and currently acting vice-president academic and provost at Brandon University. Brandon University has thriving teacher education programs at the undergraduate and graduate levels and focuses on preparing teachers for all locations with a strand that focuses on rural, Northern and First Nations, Inuit and Metis Education. With much international experience in the UK and US as well as in Canada, Heather has teaching and leadership experience both in the K-12 and post-secondary educational systems. She has published extensively in the areas of educational leadership, rural education, and online education and has presented her research in Canada, the United States, the United Kingdom, and New Zealand. She currently edits the *Rural Educator Journal*. Her passion is to engage pre- and in-service teachers in relevant and collaborative learning experiences so that they may be successful in meeting the diverse needs of the children they teach.

Susan E. Elliott-Johns is an Associate Professor and member of Graduate Faculty at Nipissing University in the Schulich School of Education, where she teaches courses and supervises graduate work in education. She is also the current Chair of

ABOUT THE CONTRIBUTORS

the Research Ethics Board. She holds a Ph.D. from McGill University, and research interests include contemporary leadership for teacher education in diverse contexts, and reflective inquiry. Susan's own reflections on experience with educational leadership for teacher education in Canada led to the inquiry that resulted in this text. Prior to joining the faculty at Nipissing in 2006 Susan enjoyed a very successful career in public education as a teacher (JK-8), literacy consultant, elementary school administrator, and teacher educator. An active member of AERA, CSSE, CATE, ISATT, and the international self-study community, she frequently provides leadership through workshops, conference presentations, keynotes, and publications for teachers, administrators, and teacher educators across Canada, Europe, the U.S., and Australia. http://www.nipissingu.ca/about-us/people/Pages/Susan-Elliott-Johns.aspx

Kimberly Franklin is Associate Professor and Dean of the School of Education at Trinity Western University. The TWU School of Education is the only teacher education program in BC that intentionally connects educational practice with the rich tradition of Christian spiritual understandings of teaching and learning. The faculty is interested in advancing educational research and educational practice that nurtures wisdom, compassion and care for all, integral and ethical ways of understanding the world and others, and transformation of learners and communities. Kimberly's research interests include the intersection of Eastern Christian spirituality with education, contemplative inquiry and pedagogy, and teacher identity/formation. She is currently on sabbatical, learning contemplative practice from experts in monasteries and completing a new edition of a book originally written by Dr. Harro Van Brummelen, *Steppingstones to Curriculum*. Her reflections on education and spirituality are regularly shared on her blog, http://educatingwithreverence.com

Rosetta Khalideen is the former Dean of the Faculty of Professional Studies at the University of the Fraser Valley, Abbotsford, British Columbia. Her portfolio included supervision of the Teacher Education Program. Rosetta began her career as a teacher in her native Guyana and later became a school administrator and a teacher educator. After migrating to Canada and completing her PhD at the University of Alberta, she worked as a faculty member and a Director at the University of Regina. Her academic career culminated in the Deanship at the University of the Fraser Valley. Rosetta has significant international education experience in the Caribbean, Panama, Thailand and Africa and one of her scholarship areas is the internationalization of higher education. She led a Tier 1 CIDA project at the University of Regina to assist the Malawi Polytechnic to develop its undergraduate and graduate technical teacher education programs. Rosetta is a recipient of the Saskatchewan Centennial medal for her contributions to education in that province.

Jane E. Lewis describes herself as a life-long educator. Jane is currently Interim Dean of the School of Professional Studies at Cape Breton University and

Associate Professor in its Department of Education. After two decades at CBU, the vast majority of which has been spent in senior leadership roles, there has been no waning of her passion for education or her mindfulness of the privilege of working in a field with such potential to positively impact the lives of individuals. Long interested in the many ways teachers make a difference and the role of teacher education in helping them do so, Jane's research and personal interests have increasingly shifted towards transformational leadership and preparing teachers as leaders of change.

Kris Magnusson joined Simon Fraser University as Dean of Education in 2009. I also served as an Associate Vice-President Academic, Associate Dean (Education) and Professor of Counselling Psychology at the University of Lethbridge (1998-2009). I started my academic journey in the Counselling Psychology program at the University of Calgary (1988-1998), and I have worked in all forms of public education in Canada, from schools (junior high teacher) to colleges, technical institutes and universities. Our Professional Development Program is known for its differentiated staffing model (employing over 40 practicing teachers each year) and for its cohort-based, integrated model of program delivery. A challenge for Teacher Education Programs everywhere is to respond to the changing dynamic of education in times of fiscal restraint. My Big Hairy Audacious Goal is for the research, teaching and community engagement of faculties of education to be recognized for the immense contributions we make to a civil and democratic society.

David Mandzuk is the Dean of the Faculty of Education at the University of Manitoba in Winnipeg, Manitoba and has been in the teaching profession for over 35 years. The teacher education program at the University of Manitoba is known for its Early, Middle, and Senior Years stream organization, its 24 weeks of practicum and, increasingly, its focus on social justice and human rights issues. David's current research and scholarly interests include teacher education reform, the foundations of education and the sociology of education. With his co-author Shelley Hasinoff, he wrote, *Slices of Life*: *Managing Dilemmas in Middle Grades Teaching* which was published by the National Middle School Association in 2010. In early 2015, he and Shelley will release their second book, this time with Oxford University Press entitled, *Case Studies in Educational Foundations: Canadian Perspectives* which will examine the myths, bandwagons, and moral panics in education.

Ken McCluskey currently serves as Dean and Professor of Education at the University of Winnipeg. Prior to taking up that position, he had 25 years experience as a school psychologist, special educator, and administrator in the public school system. A recipient of major awards for his program development, creativity, and publications from the Canadian Council for Exceptional Children, the International Centre for Innovation in Education, Reclaiming Youth International, and the World Council for Gifted and Talented Children (along with

ABOUT THE CONTRIBUTORS

his institution's teaching, research, governance, and community service awards), Ken has given in excess of 300 provincial, national, and international presentations, and has written over 100 professional articles and chapters. He is also the author, co-author, or editor of 20 books, including *Understanding ADHD: Our Personal Journey, Mentoring for Talent Development*, and *Lost Prizes: Talent Development and Problem Solving with At-Risk Students*.

James McNinch served as the Dean of the Faculty of Education at the University of Regina for a six year term, 2008-2014. He is currently the Director of the Faculty's Instructional Development and Research Unit (SIDRU) which is responsible for the management of research contracts with educational partners as well as the delivery of community-based undergraduate and graduate cohort programs in Saskatchewan and beyond. He was an active member of the Association of Canadian Deans of Education (ACDE), and was a co-author responsible for the production of the ACDE accord on Early Childhood Care and Learning (2012). In the past year, he has been a member of external review teams for Faculties of Education at U Windsor, UNB, and UBC. He also co-authored a research report, *Teacher Time* (2013) which explored the deleterious effects of various government interventions on the self-efficacy of teachers in Saskatchewan. Through camp fYrefly Saskatchewan, James remains committed in teaching, research, and service to supporting the rights of sexual and gender minority youth.

Jacqueline Muldoon is the Dean of the School of Education and Professional Learning at Trent University. She came to Trent University in Peterborough in 1983 as a faculty member in the economics department. From 1998 to 2007 she was appointed as the Director of the Business Administration program growing the program significantly with the introduction of joint majors. In 2007 she was appointed Director of the School of Education and Professional Learning, and was appointed Dean in 2010. Currently in her second term as dean, she also serves as an executive member and Vice Chair of the Ontario Association of Deans of Education. The consecutive teacher education program at Trent University builds on Trent's reputation as a leader in academically rigorous and collaborative learning. Through the use of innovative technologies, and exposure to critical research in education, students tackle contemporary issues about society, environmental sustainability and social justice in the education system. At Trent, effective teacher education is a partnership, involving the whole community as learners.

Karen Roland is currently the Acting Dean for the Faculty of Education and Academic Development at the University of Windsor. My role has been to ensure the academic vitality and operational viability of our faculty. As a change agent, I have effectively engaged faculty and staff to navigate significant programmatic changes we have faced over the past two years. I have had the sincere pleasure of teaching and learning at the University of Windsor for over 20 years in a number of challenging and rewarding positions, including: co-operative education, employment equity, experiential learning, and administration. My research interests align closely with the faculty's commitment to social justice in education and include social justice education, restorative justice, educational equity, teacher education, diversity, and educational policy and administration. I hold peer-reviewed publications, have made professional presentations, and have published teaching materials in the area of social justice and equity in education.

Ann Sherman is currently the Dean of the Faculty of Education at the University of New Brunswick. Ann started her teaching career as a high school science and math teacher after earning a B.Sc.Ed. from St. Francis Xavier university. She moved to elementary schools and earned M.Ed. degree in Leadership and then another in Curriculum and Instruction from UNB. She ended her teaching career as a school administrator before completing a Ph.D. at the University of Nottingham and moving on to teaching at the university level. She has been in university settings since 1995 and continues to research in the areas of early learning, formative assessment, inquiry-based science, the connections between all three, and the role of leadership. She is involved in numerous professional learning opportunities for in-service teachers across the Maritime provinces.

INDEX

A
Aboriginal education, 16, 62
Aboriginal perspectives, 75
Accountability, 3, 43–45, 57, 76
Achievement, viii, 8, 30, 31, 57, 82, 90, 103
Advocacym 76, 78
Authentic, 44, 73, 74, 97, 101

C
Challenges, viii, 5, 15, 25, 27–29, 32, 34, 51, 55, 58, 61, 63, 64, 67, 83, 84, 87, 91, 93, 97, 101, 102, 104
　Intrinsic, 27
　Extrinsic, 27
Change
　Process, processes, 62, 88, 90
　Transformational, 95, 100
Collaboration, 3, 24, 31, 45, 58, 71, 77, 84, 88, 95, 96
Collaborative, 32–34, 46, 52, 83, 85, 88–91, 101
Common goal, 64
Community service, 70
Competence, 21–23, 27–29, 56
Competing demands, viii, 37, 44, 99, 100
Complexities, 3, 31, 34, 73, 98–102
Complexity, vii, viii, 27, 32, 37, 81, 88, 97, 99
Constraints, 1, 32, 58, 84, 85, 99, 101
Consultative, 88, 89, 91, 99
Critical pedagogy, 9, 83, 100

D
Deans, vii, viii, 1–5, 13–15, 30–32, 34, 43, 44, 46, 61–64, 75, 76, 94, 95, 97–101, 103, 104

Decision-making processes, 2, 5, 33, 84, 85
Differentiation, 13, 14, 15, 17, 81, 84, 87, 90, 101

E
Educational change, 1, 3, 46, 50, 55
Engagement, 3, 32, 56, 57, 83, 88, 89, 101, 103
Epistemology, 9
Equity, 45, 83, 84, 89
Expectations, viii, 1, 5, 34, 44, 77, 95, 101, 103
Expertise, 5, 9, 82, 83, 85

F
Faculties of education, 1–3, 15, 17, 34, 61, 62, 76, 77, 81, 87, 97, 99, 100
First Nations, 7–10, 75

G
Global, vii, 3, 23, 49, 51, 52, 68, 70, 77, 84, 88, 89, 99, 102
Graduate studies, 10, 17
Guiding principles, 68, 81, 83, 102

I
In-service, 58, 76, 83
Indigenous, 7–10, 75, 100
Indigenous teacher education, 7, 97, 101
Insights, 1–5, 97, 99, 102, 104
Innovation, viii, 1, 31, 33, 43–46, 51, 84

L
Leaders, 1–5, 7, 19, 25, 30, 32, 38, 40, 44, 46, 52, 55, 64, 77, 83, 85, 88, 98–100, 102–104

113

INDEX

Leadership
  Academic, 1, 25
  Administrative, 30, 98
  Change, 37, 50
  Effective, 82, 83, 97, 99
Learning, viii, 3, 4, 8, 26–28, 31, 33, 40, 43–46, 49, 50, 55–58, 68–70, 73–75, 77, 82, 83, 87–89, 93–96, 98–100, 102, 103, 105
Learning community, 26, 75
Local, vii, 52, 68, 89, 95, 98, 104

M
Multiple perspectives, 2, 5, 95, 97

N
Neo-liberal, neo-liberal agenda, 73, 78, 101–103

O
Organizational culture, 31–34, 98

P
Partners, 40, 75, 76
  Internal, 86
  External, 86
Partnership(s), 45, 46, 61, 70, 81–86, 98
Pedagogy, 2–5, 9, 29, 49, 74, 83, 88, 89, 100, 103, 104
Policymakers, 5, 77
Politics, 14, 46, 70, 77, 101, 103, 104
Politics of care, 96
Pre-service, 8, 33, 49, 58, 68, 74, 76, 77, 93–96, 103
Pre-service programs, 3, 4, 83, 84
Preferred future, 5, 56–58
Professional development, 28, 59, 75, 76
Professional identity, 73
Professional learning, 58, 83, 104, 105
Program renewal, 74–76, 103

Public education, 55, 57, 73, 76, 77

Q
Quality, vii, 13, 29, 37, 39, 40, 51, 57, 58, 63, 68, 84, 87

R
Reflection(s), 2, 3, 5, 10, 28, 30, 37, 67, 70, 77, 81, 83, 95, 97, 100, 103
Reform, educational reform, 1, 2, 29, 43, 45, 46, 49, 77, 97
Relationship(s), viii, 10, 26–28, 31, 46, 51, 52, 55, 57, 68, 69, 75, 77, 81–83, 95, 98, 99, 101, 104
Researchers, 5, 103
Resources, 8, 27, 30, 33, 37, 45, 46, 57, 58, 62, 63, 77, 84
Restructuring, 19, 24, 25, 30, 33, 34, 85, 98, 102, 103

S
School system, 3, 49, 69, 97, 99
Schools, vii, 7, 8, 10, 25–27, 34, 37, 43–45, 50, 70, 74, 76, 78, 93–96, 99, 100
Scrutiny, 1, 44, 63, 99
Service learning, 68, 69, 75, 89
Shared experience, 39
Shared responsibility, 46, 82, 83, 85, 98, 101
Situated contexts, 3, 100, 103
Skills, vii, viii, 26, 31, 34, 44–46, 74, 76, 83, 84
Social justice, 67, 73, 74, 76, 83, 84, 89, 97, 101–103
Stakeholders, vii, 1, 3, 5, 28, 33, 44, 46, 61, 62, 64, 75, 82, 83, 95–97, 100, 101, 103
Standardized testing, 77
Success, 7, 8, 25, 31, 33, 34, 52, 56–58, 70, 73, 75, 76, 89, 93–95, 98, 99
Succession planning, 61, 64, 100, 104

Support, viii, 9, 25, 28–30, 40, 44, 46, 49–51, 57, 62, 64, 68, 70, 73, 76, 78, 82, 89, 91, 93, 95, 99, 100, 104, 105
Survival, 69, 81, 87
Sustainability, 51, 70
Sustainable leadership, 102, 104, 105

T

Teacher education change, 1–3, 87, 88
Teacher educators, vii, viii, 2, 37, 52, 89, 94, 97, 99
Teacher preparation, vii, 27, 44–46, 50, 95
Teacher-training, 9, 25, 26, 28, 29, 73
Teachers, vii, 2, 3, 7–9, 13–16, 25, 27–29, 31, 34, 43, 45, 49–52, 55, 56, 59, 61, 62, 67–70, 73–78, 85, 87, 93–96, 99, 100, 102, 103
Teaching, vii, viii, 1, 3, 4, 7–10, 14–17, 27–29, 33, 34, 37, 43, 45, 49, 51, 52, 55–59, 64, 70, 73–75, 77, 82, 83, 87, 88, 93, 99–100
Technology(ies), 16, 43–46, 50–52, 55–57, 74, 76, 77, 84, 100
Transitions, 1, 2, 4, 14, 59, 97
Trust, 31, 32, 46, 82, 85, 91, 98
Twenty-first century learning, viii, 1–3, 43–46, 52, 73, 83, 87, 89, 104

V

Vision, vii, 3–5, 7–10, 14, 17, 23, 24, 29, 30, 33, 37, 39, 40, 45, 46, 52, 61, 64, 76, 82, 83, 89, 91, 98, 100, 102
Voices, 1–3, 5, 39, 46, 85, 90, 96, 97, 100, 104

CPSIA information can be obtained
at www.ICGtesting.com
Printed in the USA
FFOW04n1404151015
17728FF

9 789462 099302